THE
HOPE
FILLED
MARRIAGE

Every marriage starts with a purpose
Every purpose is fueled by vision
Every vision is fulfilled through hope

Kevin and Christine Meland, MSW

Veritas
Communications

Veritas Communications, Inc.

www.VeritasIncorporated.com

For information about special discounts for
bulk purchases or to schedule author interviews
or other public relations events, please call:
(951) 587–1135 or (719) 275–7775
or email us at:
info@VeritasIncorporated.com

This book is dedicated to our children

To our son Brandon, you're effusive, gregarious, and rock solid. Who could have known that God would rescue us in our mess of a marriage and give us a chance to parent you again? Thanks for giving us the opportunity to fumble through at times. We loved raising you, watching you, and now being a part of your grand adventure of adulthood. Your life is before you, live it with honor. You are a leader and a seeker of truth. Our lives are richer because of you.

Our daughter Kaisha, you have added a dimension of depth to our lives, and our second marriage, that is unparalleled. In you we see clearly the differences between the sexes. You are all a princess should be and we only pray and hope we raise you to be a woman of deep inner character as well as outward beauty. You are a deep well and God adorns you with grace.

Our daughter Lilliana, you are a fireball, an adventurer, and a well packaged surprising gift from God. You epitomize tenacity. We see this as a demonstration of your fight for all that you want, and we pray and hope we give you an opportunity to use that fight for the kingdom of God. Your life is ever before you and our lives are much richer and funnier because of you.

May you all know that your parents sought the great hope found in Jesus Christ to fuel our marriage and our relationship with you, our children. We know you too will have hope filled lives and hope filled marriages.

Contents

14

Acknowledgements

Thank you Lord for what you did in our marriage. How you possibly pulled at our hearts and helped us rebuild our broken marriage is still a miracle. We are celebrating almost ten years of remarriage and your Hope still compels us. May we always honor you with our lives.

Thank you to our parents. Mom and Dad Meland, thank you so much for helping build hope in my life by leading through the example of your spiritual walk and your life long commitment to one another. Thank you also for believing in me, your son, even when I failed in so many ways. You guys are my champions. Mom and Dad Richey, you have triumphed over much pain and used hope to bring healing to your own respective lives and your life as a couple. You live in hope daily and your support and love motivate us.

Thank you to the board of directors for Mountain Haven Marriage Ministry for supporting the vision we have to impart hope to couples all over the world. Thank you to the multiple people that caught a vision for

Mountain Haven and who support the ministry of touching marriages through your financial, prayer, emotional, and spiritual support. You make this possible. Thank you to our concise editor; Jermaine Matthews–you are a true cheerleader. We love you.

Preface

How do you build a stronger foundation of hope in a good marriage? How do you love your spouse again after you find out they committed adultery? How do you wake up day after day when you feel like you are in an empty shell marriage? How do you keep trying when the pain of disappointment has a stranglehold on your heart? How do you have the courage to love again after a divorce? All change starts with hope. Why did the fallen world need Jesus? Because we needed hope– an anticipation, expectation, or a chance to be redeemed. Marriage, today more then ever, needs hope. We need to expect, prospect, or see the possibility of God's best within our relationship. Without that, and without the vision for what our marriage can look like, we wither, we shut down, we explode, we seek solace from others, and we divorce, sometimes physically but most often in our hearts.

So why read this book? Why have hope if your spouse isn't willing to change? That is why hope is essential. The power of hope allows you to see what you may bring to the relationship, and how you may impact your spouse; it takes the focus off of your spouse and onto yourself. If your ultimate hope is in Jesus, you are able to see truthfully what needs to change in your life first and then in respect to how you react to your spouse or their specific issues or struggles. Then if two people can tap into the power of hope and vision for their lives, they can live out a marriage where both are growing. God wants them to grow, together, but ever sharpening the other person into maturity. This is a book meant to challenge you in ways you may have let something other then hope, perhaps dread, despair or disappointment rule how you view your marriage relationship; and if you have, how hope can be renewed again.

Many people want to read a book written by experts in their field. So what makes us experts you may ask? We live each moment by hope but more importantly we understand the power of hope to heal, reconcile, and help us move forward every day in our marriage. We were divorced in 1998. It was bitter, ugly, and painful. The eight years of our marriage prior to that were riddled with every possible failure a marriage could experience and we had hurt each other beyond repair (or so we thought). We were hopeless by all standards of the word. It was difficult to even talk to one another and we left scars on one another's hearts that from a world's standard were unforgivable. The idea of co–parenting and trying to get along was impossible.

Then the power of hope to bring change began to germinate in one of us. Kevin got a revelation of God's love for him and the promise of hope to save his life after all the destructive choices he had made, including leaving his family. He pursued Chris to ask for forgiveness and seek a better parenting relationship. In doing this he planted seeds of hope in her heart. Hope germinates if *you* allow it to and that is what happened with Chris. She received the hope she needed to try again.

After one year of divorce we were miraculously remarried in 1999, and have been pursuing a hope filled marriage since then. In that vein, in 2007, we started Mountain Haven Marriage & Family Reconciliation Ministry, a non–profit marriage ministry dedicated to healing marriages in crisis all over the world. We are also developing this book to be used in a seminar format in churches across the nation. We moved the home base of this ministry to the beautiful Rocky Mountains in Canon City, Colorado in June 2008, and in the near future plan to build a ministry retreat center to minister to couples right in our own home. We are full time marriage ministers. So are we experts? Well, we are skilled at keeping hope alive, we are definitely practiced at the art of hope, and we walk in authority because we live the message. So *yes,* by the grace of God we are. We want this message to impart hope to you and empower you to go deeper in your marriage than you may have imagined. Or for those of you wanting to see if you can make it work again, read on and know that ***through Christ,*** all things are possible. We are living proof of that.

How to Use This Book and Study Guide

This book is designed to be read by individuals, couples, or as a group study. It can be used as a devotional for couples seeking a closer relationship or as a group study led by a couple leaders at a church setting. However you choose to use it, our prayer is that you take time for each reading and then **really reflect and answer the questions following the chapter reading.** The reading is meant to set up the chapter idea and to get you thinking about the topic as it specifically relates to your marriage relationship. As a group process you can shorten or lengthen the weeks of study depending on the time commitment of your group. We have chosen to combine the reading and the study guide together so there is a flow and rhythm to your study, and so you don't have to switch gears to look at questions in a separate study guide. It is best read chapter by chapter rather then a portion of the chapter. But however you choose to use it, just be clear with your expectations of the group or yourself.

This book is for marriages of any age group, or any faith level. It is written to challenge any marriage and any person if they will let it. Your hope does not have to be gone or even dwindling to pick this book up. If however your hope is simply gone, this book may also help you decide if you can hope again in your marriage. The key idea is to read it with an open heart for change. There will be questions at the end of each chapter and then a "Hope Challenge" that is meant to stretch you out of your routine, habits, and comfort zone. Each change you make in your heart, attitude, or mind can bring hope to your situation until it becomes a lifestyle and you are continually filled with Hope on a daily basis no matter what your circumstances may be. So dig in and strive right now to grasp hope and never let it go.

Chapter 1 – A Foundation of Hope

"For I know the thoughts that I think toward you, says the Lord, thoughts of peace and not of evil, to give you a future and a hope." Jeremiah 29:11 NKJV

Think about an engine trying to run without oil. Or how about playing a piano without ever tuning it. We know it can be done, right? But the end result is disaster. The engine seizes up and the piano fails to play notes that resemble music. That is like your marriage without hope. Hope is defined as "a feeling of expectation and desire for a certain thing to happen, grounds for believing that something good may happen, and a feeling of trust," in the New Oxford American Dictionary. The Hebrew and Greek definitions range from "expectancy", "a place of refuge", "trust", "to anticipate", "security" and "safety".

There are many instructions in the Word of God about how husbands and wives must live and fulfill their respective roles, but there are times when we all need to refuel our spirits in living out those roles. That is where hope comes in. Hope gives you the fuel you need to fulfill being the husband or wife you want to be, and God desires you to be. Hope builds a foundation, but it also strengthens the foundation of a marriage.

Hope is Just a Feeling, Isn't it?

If hope were just a feeling we conjured up in the hard times it would be easy to make it through those difficult times. But hope is often the result of hard times. Or better yet, hope is often borne through adversity. If you are struggling in your marriage, if it looks like failure is imminent and you feel you've been hurt

> *Jesus brought hope to a broken and fallen world by giving Himself up for* it

beyond repair, then you need more than a feeling, don't you? The heart can conjure up all sorts of feelings and emotions to get us through difficult times but hope is an outpouring of pure expectation based on Jesus Himself. Jesus brought hope to a broken and fallen world by giving Himself up for us. So essentially hope cannot be a feeling. It is actually an action. An active anticipation based on truth, that not only gets us through the difficult times, but also empowers us to make different decisions during those times that are not just emotion based.

If Jesus himself was the living hope, He functioned with the bigger picture in mind. Ultimately His picture included His sacrifice but He always knew the prize beyond the circumstances. How did He do that? He kept that hope always before Him that His death and resurrection would save us. How do we allow hope to work for us? We keep in mind that our first hope, the one we had when we married, when we believed the best about our future with our spouse, is powerful to cause change in our life and in the life of our spouse. How? Losing hope affects everything; thoughts first, then attitude, and then actions. Does an affair actually just happen the way we hear about it? You meet someone at work and find yourself drawn to him or her and then suddenly you are in the midst of a torrid love affair? No way. Affairs are complex but ultimately the loss of hope starts a cycle that causes us to look elsewhere for places to fill us up. If you have lost the expectancy of a certain response from your spouse it seems easier to just look for someone, or something else that fills that up so much easier.

Anticipation is Powerful

If one of our definitions of hope is anticipation then what does it mean to anticipate? To expect, wait for, or predict. If we already expect a certain response from our spouse, then disappointment comes much more readily. For instance, because we have had so many disputes about finances, we have grown accustomed to a certain level of conflict

> Unfortunately, most of us start patterns that embed in our brains, imprint on our souls, and even establish themselves in our physical reactions to one another.

whenever we discuss money. Kevin anticipates that I will be disappointed in him so he anticipates my response as one of irritation and lack of respect. Now sometimes I am disrespectful and downright irritated about the conversation, but since our remarriage I have tried to respond differently and listen more and respond less. The power of anticipation has created a dynamic between us that means we have to work hard in this area to deliberately listen. If we can successfully get through multiple discussions about finances without high conflict, we change our anticipation, or hope level, for the next time.

Unfortunately, most of us start patterns that embed in our brains, imprint on our souls, and even establish themselves in our physical reactions to one another. Our brains immediately think the thoughts we are accustomed to thinking about that person: "he is such a bad manager of finances" or "she is so emotional". Our soul gets involved by stirring up emotions like frustration, despair, rejection, or anger and then our bodies react in kind by causing our heart to race,

> Many of the responses *of hopelessness* are founded in previous family of origin experiences

our stomach to hurt, and our fists to clench. We are told in Romans 12:2 *"And do not be conformed to this world but be transformed by the renewing of your mind that you may prove what is that good and acceptable and perfect will of God."* NKJV

It all starts with our thoughts. Transforming our minds means actually altering, changing, or distorting our mind. So in other words, the thoughts we think may not be the thoughts that God *wants* us to think. They may be thoughts that come because pain is associated with that particular experience. The pain in marriage is typically not just the result of failed interactions with our spouse year after year. Many of the responses *of hopelessness* are founded in previous family of origin experiences. So for me, Chris, I grew up in poverty with no father and always feeling unprotected and uncared for. There is a root deep inside of me that says I will never be taken care of. With that type of expectation inside I anticipate the same responses from Kevin time and time again whenever we talk about money. How can I change my hope level in this situation? Start anticipating a change within myself first. I am not living in my childhood; I am able to handle financial changes more maturely. I am protected and cared for by God, my heavenly Father. Even if Kevin were to continually disappoint, I can anticipate myself changing in response to it because my Hope is in Christ not a person. *Did you hear that? My hope is not in my spouse, it is in CHRIST JESUS!*

The real joy comes when both people are willing to make changes to minister to the family of origin hurts in the other person. Unfortunately what we so often do is marry someone similar to our mother or father and then spend the rest of our married life trying to change that person. What actually brings about permanent change is when we see that part of our spouse that is flawed and we pray and minister to it. We respond less to the flaws and anticipate what God is doing in that person's life. Is this easy? Absolutely not! *It takes hope* and it takes a strong commitment to *your* marriage and to the Lord. Anticipating that those irritating qualities within your spouse may become less irritating is impossible. But, anticipating that God will reveal to you different and unique ways to love your spouse is wholly possible. This is when hope is able to do its work within us. We again have the strength because of hope to interact about painful situations with our spouse. Proverbs 10:28 states *"The hope of the righteous will be gladness: but the expectation of the wicked will perish."* NKJV

Hope helps us do more than just hang on in despair. It allows us to have joy and gladness in the process of waiting for change.

If our hope is in Christ then it is possible to wake up every day and trust that God will do His work in our spouse despite our own negative encounters with them. Our gladness is a result of our continual trust in God's goodness. If we expect that God is at work within us and within our spouse then the result will be gladness. It says in the passage above, "the hope of the righteous." It is clear there is an expectation that our lives will be righteous before God in order to access His hope. Many of us read

> *If we desire to grow, to change, to keep believing the best about our situation and our spouse, we will be open to change and open to help*

that and think we need to be perfect ourselves. The key with Christ is always the heart. A thorough examination of your heart will reveal unrighteousness or sin, especially as it relates to your spouse. There are some things that we must look at deeper that block hope. They are patterned responses or beliefs we have in our lives towards our spouse, but these responses are sinful and therefore unrighteous. They may be blocking hope and as we explore deeper in the chapters to follow we must identify those things in order to let hope work for us in our marriage.

Desire is Central to Change

Desire is also a synonym for hope as well as a key component to living in hope. If we desire to grow, to change, to keep believing the best about our situation and our spouse, we will be open to change and open to help. If however our desire has been quenched through years of hurtful experiences with our spouse, we stop believing in change because we stop desiring it. That is what happened in our marriage. We kept up patterns of anger, hurt, and insecurity. It prevented us from understanding our roles in the relationship. Kevin lost his desire to be a spiritual leader because I disrespected him so often. Instead of him pressing in deeper and staying the course in faithfulness, he succumbed to feelings of despair. He lost hope and his desire was quenched and the result was unrighteous behavior that resulted in our divorce. I was so disgusted with his inability to lead, and his constant passivism, that I allowed myself to start verbalizing condemnation and failure to him. I spoke of divorce often as a solution to our problems. I had my hope in him to change, not in Christ to change him or myself. I only focused on the behaviors, not how I was responding to them. I was building up a wall of protection and hurt, which I wasn't even able to hope for any bit of change. So even when there was change it couldn't last because our defenses wouldn't allow desire to cultivate within us and continue to press toward lasting and real change.

The only way to keep desire fed is to keep pressing towards the vision, the hope that God intended for your marriage. It will lead to a softening of your heart as well as the heart of your spouse. Remember, if the hope of the righteous is happiness, then happiness is possible. When you have a spouse that lets you down continually and disappoints you, it is easy to fall into unrighteous thoughts, and eventually unrighteous acts. First is the thought, "I deserve better", "This isn't the person I married", or "I hate the way that person acts", and eventually elevating to those thoughts, "We should just get a divorce. Our kids would be better off rather then listening to all our fighting." Friends, these thoughts have the power to quench desire. Once desire is quenched, action in the affirmative becomes almost impossible. Whereas action to support our thoughts is second nature and if our thoughts are continually negative, these thoughts will most often result in an action that supports our hurt feelings. Ultimately then reaffirming our negative thoughts.

Hope fuels desire and desire is the starting point. We often times give up on getting help stating, "They won't go to counseling", or "They don't go to church", again, our hope is in the person we married, not in Christ and it is weak, at the very least. A desire to continue to grow in Christ, and to love an unlovable spouse, takes hope. The hope motivates a desire to action, and when you see the need for change you will be the first to act on it for yourself even with an unwilling spouse.

Getting hope back takes an inner recognition of the role you may have played in the relationship. Hope fails us when we look primarily at the other person's failures and shortcomings in the marriage, rather then take an honest assessment of what we may have done to contribute to the mess. Since real hope is found in the example of Jesus Christ we need only to look to His life example for guidance. When all else failed and His disciples slept while He prayed, Jesus had to press forward and seek help to maintain His strength. *At that point I'm sure it would have been easier to give up and lose hope in humanity, but instead,* He sought help from His father God and cried out to Him to continue to strengthen Him for the task at hand; His crucifixion. Maybe you need to seek help from God because you can't face the task at hand; your marriage. Perhaps bitterness has crept in so deep you feel you no longer even love your spouse. Maybe you are secretly having emotional conversations with someone at work because they really seem to understand you. Perhaps you are even having a physical relationship with that person. Maybe you are shopping too much, or looking at pornography, or throwing yourself into work far too many hours. There is a whole list of things we choose to do that we will discuss in detail in the next chapters. These things may be quenching hope, masking hope and therefore all you anticipate and all you desire is seen through the framework of your own sinful choices. That is a pretty bleak view and it is based on a faulty paradigm.

Recognizing how you are falling short yourself and taking the time to actually seek help and change, is the gateway to renewing hope and fueling desire. All too often our focus is on recognizing how our spouse is falling short. We can attest to the power of this type of thinking based on our own experience in our first marriage. While I focused on Kevin's passivity, bad financial

> *All too often our focus is on recognizing how our spouse is falling short*

choices, and his lack of spiritual leadership: I nitpicked everything, the messy garage, the watching of NFL football rather then talking to me, and the way he talked to our son. I was overly sensitive and hyper critical because I had truly lost hope. Rather than seeking counsel and support for myself I criticized Kevin for not initiating counseling for us. Rather than just saying no to the financial decisions that I had control over, I stormed around making a scene and ranting about how I gave everything up for him only to support his flagrant financial decisions.

I had lost desire to change myself in the marriage. I had no hope for us as a couple, I saw only the "mismatch" that we were and felt hopeless. I constantly anticipated his next moves, and trust me, none of those moves were anticipated to be done right. Until he actually said "I can do nothing right and I'm a failure." He definitely had no desire to go to counseling then. What was the point, if only to further amplify what he already knew: he was a dismal failure and so was our marriage. The desire for help was then, not motivated out of hope, but out of obligation. Since both of us were living pretty selfishly without really caring about our own righteousness, there was no happiness. There was no real change because there was no inner conviction to change ourselves first. We only sought to change the other person's flaws, believing that if they would only change we could be happy. We approached counseling with that belief system and it failed because we measured the outcome by our happiness with our spouse's behaviors, not by evaluating the changes within our own hearts.

You see, in the beginning it was not that way. We married with idealism. Kevin knew about my past without a stable father and provider, and with many hurts. I married him wanting to help support him as a man and as a leader, knowing he struggled with boldness and leadership. I loved his gentleness because it meant he was kind and loving. I didn't know that his gentleness would eventually become passivity in my vernacular, nor did he know that my independence would become control and bitterness. For hope to succeed one of us would have needed to fuel the fire of our original desire towards one another. He wanted to minister to me over the loss of a father, over the poverty, and the abuse in my past. I wanted to help him grow in leadership and strength by supporting him and speaking in love towards him. When one of us chose to hurt the other one in the beginning, there was forgiveness, there was kindness, and there was hope. We moved towards change because of our desire to grow as a couple. But once the breakdown occurred in one of us, and it didn't matter, the perception of what our marriage was, also changed. If Kevin was not gentle, I nagged him. He chose to see me as a malicious, controlling wife rather then believe in the hope we once had, that we were meant for one another because God would use us to grow each other in Christ. No longer did God bring us together to love one another unconditionally, to minister to one another by seeing the hurt inside that person and reaching towards it rather then repelling away from it. We now perceived our marriage as unhappy. There was a grand canyon of space between us. We had lost hope for God's original plan for us and we were doing it all in our own strength, our own desire, and our own love. It was not love motivated by God's hope; it was love motivated by performance. We only had hope if things went well, if we didn't get in a fight, if Kevin led by having us go to church, and if I didn't snap at him. Our desire was only motivated by the other person's external behavior not by God's infinite wisdom to help us grow, and have His hope, despite difficult circumstances.

Let's face it, a spouse that performs to our standard is much easier to live with and find hope with than the spouse that lets us down through their choices and behaviors. This is why we all need hope. Christ centered hope will motivate us through those difficult times. And hope that is continually filled up in marriage is a hope that helps us learn how to anticipate our spouse's responses differently in order to prepare for change, and it is a hope that will give us the desire for the needed changes within ourselves and an openness towards the changes our spouse desires.

Taking it Home

1.) What hopes or ideals do you recall having when you married your spouse? How have those changed over the years and why?

2.) Answer honestly, what is your hope level for real change in your marriage? On a scale of 1–10, 1 being no hope and 10 being extremely hopeful? How does that compare with your spouse?

3.) What is one thing you can identify that you say to yourself, or a behavior you do, that is contributing to your loss of hope in your marriage? What can you do to change that today? (Be honest here– i.e. tell my spouse, tell a friend, get counseling, do a word study on this particular issue, etc..)

4.) Name one behavior or response that you anticipate from your spouse (especially during conflict) that may be stopping you from seeing any real change in them? (Be specific) What is something very specific that you can say or do to seek clarity or change your anticipation level? (i.e. stop interrupting them, be silent, talk more, etc)

5.) In order to fuel your desire for a better marriage there may be some choices you are currently making that you need to let go of. Can you identify any thing you are doing or acting on that has affected your desire for change in your marriage? What is it? (talking negative to others, talking divorce, shutting down) Would you be willing to share it with your spouse? Is it something that requires outside help? If so what help will you seek?

HOPE CHALLENGE

Think of one thing today that you know will bring hope into your spouse's life (i.e. flowers, card, letter, a hug, a gift, a movie, quality time, fixing something in the house, helping out with a job) do something small everyday this week to create a hopeful atmosphere around your spouse.

Chapter 2 – Identifying and Dealing with Hope Busters – Part 1

"Hope deferred makes the heart sick, but when the desire comes it is a tree of life." Proverbs 13:12 NKJV

"When hope is crushed, the heart is crushed, but a wish come true fills you with joy." MSG

So we know why hope and the power of hope is important, but most of us also know the power of broken hope, or broken dreams. The feeling of hopelessness is a constricting force that threatens to steal our joy and rob our motivation and "feelings" of love towards our spouse. Obviously we cannot live by feelings and some of the actions in marriage are done because of commitment or marital duty. But friends, if you are living the majority of your married life going through the actions of marital obligation, it is time for you to check your heart, check your hope level, and truly evaluate if you have cast aside your hopes, plans, and desires for your marriage and settled for surviving instead.

In breaking down Proverbs 13:12, we see that hope is deferred is also hope that is late, overdue, or postponed. It makes our heart sick and our heart is the seat of our emotions and feelings. Now we believe we are called to live by a higher, more spiritually guided standard rather then being driven by our hearts wants, but ultimately we also know the outcome of two people being guided by the Spirit and not guided by emotions can result in marital satisfaction and marital happiness. When we are not depending on our spouse's actions to feed our emotional needs and define our hope level, but rather we are doing actions to please the Lord, it is more than likely that our hope will not be deferred. That doesn't mean we won't experience disappointment. It means we are able to see the holes in our hope and take action before soul sickness is reached.

Hope Busters Create a Wounded Soul

Unfortunately for the majority of us we had a hope, a vision, and an expectation of our spouse or our marriage and we didn't take action before our souls experienced a wound. These wounds can vary from the gaping hole of infidelity and betrayal, the anguish of spousal neglect, the scars from perpetual negative words spoken against you from a spouse, and the emptiness of believing that you and your spouse are growing apart. We call the issues that

> The power of the tongue to speak life and death is recorded in the Bible multiple times

drive hope away and cause a person to lose hope, hope busters. We named a few above, but there are many different reasons we can identify as couples that have stolen our hope. The purpose of this chapter is to identify hope busters, really articulate what they may look like in marriage, and evaluate strategies to overcome them and renew hope. As you look at these, we want you to know we have identified many of them from our own marriage as well as from listening to other couples identify the hope busters they have experienced. There is no shame in admitting to allowing any one or all of these to invade and affect your marriage relationship. If we were to answer honestly, we can identify almost every one of these as an issue for us in our first marriage, prior to divorce. Because of how many hope busters we want to extrapolate on, we will break it up into parts 1 and 2. We are going to start with the smaller, but not insignificant hope busters and build to the bigger, more complex ones.

Negative Words

The power of the tongue to speak life and death is recorded in the Bible multiple times (see Psalm 34, Proverbs 10, and James 3). All of us can recall hurtful and vicious words spoken against us by a friend, family member or spouse. Again we look at the soul, and the impact of words to build up the emotions or tear them down. Take an honest inventory about how you talk. Language and words are not just phonetic structures you allow to fall out of your brain. Words have power and when we wield them we are using them because of their affiliation to us. So when Kevin says things like, "I can't ever make you happy," in response to an argument we are having about something, he is affiliating or connecting meaning to that response. I may not even be saying that he can't make me happy. But he knows from our first marriage that he has disappointed me so many times and I was never quiet about telling him, so he now has a powerful negative affiliation to conflict. His first response is, "I can't make you happy," when the situation may be calling just for a listening ear and I do not actually need anything from him in regards to happiness. The negative words, "I can never make you happy," if said over and over again are believed and accepted as truth in our relationship until he convinces himself to stop trying to bring happiness to our relationship and I eventually stop expecting it.

There are also the negative words we use that are so much a part of us we may have lost our sense that they are negative any longer. Here are a few examples, "You never do ....", "You always do......", You're a bad listener"," Why did we ever get married?" "We should get a divorce", "We aren't going to make it", "We weren't meant to be", "Your not the person I married", and then of course the standard name calling that some of the more expressive couples, such as ourselves, resort to. Name–calling is not just expletives, or crassness. It can also be subtle and cunning.

Negative words are listed as a smaller hope buster, but we must stress that besides thoughts, which lead to words, this is one of the biggest open doors in any relationship. The Word says in Hebrews 12:14–15,

"Pursue peace with all people, and holiness without which no one will see the Lord: looking carefully lest anyone fall short of the grace of God; lest any root of bitterness springing up cause trouble, and by this many become defiled." NKJV

There is one sure way for a bitter root to grow and that is through words. They are the water for the bitterness. Be aware that bitterness is a poison. There are some poisons that are slow to take affect because they build up in the bloodstream but they cannot be detected in a blood test. This is like the bitterness that has taken root for so long that it becomes a part of your very personhood. These are often times expressed in snide comments, having a sick feeling when you are around that person, feeling like your skin is crawling, finding that you are judging every move that person makes, and a general dissatisfaction in that person's presence. Bitterness is the vilest of strongholds because it can completely sap hope and destroy any expectation or desire for future changes. The strategy against bitterness can begin for you by asking the Lord to reveal to you where you may have let bitterness come in. This is a difficult process and takes honest soul searching. If you can find someone you trust and who will support you, then confess this stronghold to them, and then finally seek forgiveness from the person you harbor it towards. If this is a person that will not receive you or will mock your efforts, then choose an alternative route like a letter or using a third person to facilitate conversation.

Remember you can't control the person's response to you but you are working towards shutting down negative words and bridling your own tongue (See James 1). So no matter how they respond or receive you, you can change your interaction by having a different statement ready in response. If you need to write out a few statements that are opposite of your "typical" negative response then you should do that and practice it, as well as ask the Lord to help you be creative. It will take time, so don't get discouraged. Words are something we will battle with throughout our lives but winning this battle bit by bit is possible and very rewarding.

> Bitterness is the vilest of strongholds because it can completely sap hope and destroy any expectation or desire for future changes

Irritations/Personality Differences

You are probably thinking how could personality differences cause me to lose hope in my marriage? Let's look at a spectrum of personality issues that we may confront in a spouse. One of you is a night person and one is a morning person, and it is incredibly annoying when you want to talk about the kids as you are getting ready for bed and your spouse falls asleep on you. Or how about the person who is completely disorganized with paperwork and the other spouse has a file for everything. Then there is the introvert who doesn't like social situations and yet you are a social butterfly. Perhaps you find yourself living with a person who loves TV and you would rather be on the go. What if you love exercise and your spouse would rather lie on the couch. Maybe you want to get involved with a group at church but your spouse is a loner and doesn't want you to leave the home. Time after time if you ask your spouse to change a habit that you believe will be helpful to the relationship, it can really disappoint, and even hurt you if they don't see the need for it. Worse yet is if they see the problem but just won't make the change.

For us this played out in many ways. A really important one was where we took vacations. Kevin always wanted to go West for every vacation and I always wanted to go East or somewhere tropical. In our first marriage we spent every family vacation at a national park in the western states. The personality issue is that Kevin is much more scheduled and less flexible. I am flexible and adventurous, wanting to try a lot of different places. However, I also struggled with not knowing how to ask him to give me what I wanted because I had the father hole inside. Therefore, I always deferred to Kevin. When I told him later how I felt, his response was, "Well you like the West also so what is the difference?" The difference was personality. I started to feel so irritated and angry that he always got his way. His personality seemed overpowering and controlling and my hope level was greatly diminished. In our second marriage, this is an issue we talked about quite extensively and the bottom line is that I just needed to be more clear and more persistent and tell him even though I like his idea I want to do mine. Because of that change we have been able to go on two tropical vacations and Kevin would really like to plan a trip out East in the near future!

It is hard to admit that your spouse could possibly irritate you, but if we are honest there are irritations that can really rob you of your joy and your spouse may have some of those characteristics. The honest and best way to deal with these is to understand that every one of us has irritating qualities and the way that we are helped is through someone lovingly helping us see other possible alternatives to how we deal with issues. Getting to the root of why your spouse may really irritate you helps you understand that some pet peeves are based on negative life experiences with a person who may have dealt with you that way. If you can identify where the root of that irritation is, it could be a breakthrough for you and your spouse. If you are feeling your hope very diminished because of irritating qualities of your spouse, we would first encourage you to sit down and tell your spouse what it is you are hurting from and pray about it together so that you can forgive and let go. Sometimes it is helpful to take a personality inventory like the Meyers Briggs to understand that some characteristics are hard wired into certain types of personalities. Understanding that some of your spouse's irritating characteristics are common to many people could help you have more grace. It is not imperative to tell your spouse every time they irritate you, but it is important to not let these irritations build up until you feel there is no hope for change for either you or your spouse.

Feeling Incompatible/Belief That We Are Growing Apart

What always amazes us is how many people we meet that get married and have a couple kids and a few years later decide they are not compatible. Or one of them is busy building a career and the other is taking care of kids and they suddenly feel like they are living in different worlds. This is one of the most common complaints of many couples and in fact was one of the driving forces behind our own divorce. We both believed that we were completely incompatible and that we actually were so far apart that nothing could bring us back together.

> *We just believed, like most couples do, that we were polar opposites on every issue*

There are many different meanings of the word incompatible including: ill suited, mismatched, irreconcilable, contrary, opposing, clashing, contradictory, and antagonistic. These are not words that we used when we were dating and surprisingly these words only started to feel normal the more our opinions differed, the more exhausted we got with trying to explain the same thing over and over to our spouse, and the more changes that came in our life. We didn't stop to consider,

"As iron sharpens iron so man sharpens the countenance of his friend." Proverbs 27:17 NKJV

We just believed, like most couples do, that we were polar opposites on every issue. The reality is that every stage of life brings with it changes and with those changes different responses from you and your spouse towards those changes. As we respond to these changes in ways that vary from one another it can really start to get irritating watching how your spouse responds in ways that don't make sense to you. Again these experiences just feed the sense that you're drifting apart from your spouse. The more complex our lives become as couples, the more intricate and multifaceted our issues and struggles become. Whether it is dealing with career changes, how having kids changes your perspective, dealing with aging parents, or moving multiple times; these experiences lend themselves to the temptation to feel distant from your spouse. In our lives this was a belief system that we really bought into especially since we got married young. However, this is not an issue just for those that marry young. It is an issue that carries over as we progress through differing stages and losses in our lives. If we don't pull together, moving as one unit through change, we start to drift and live independently of our covenant with our spouse.

I went to college and worked while we were married and Kevin and I grew more and more distant because of my desire to attend college. I was in a world of academics; he was in a blue–collar world where his work ended when he got home. We had so many terrible fights about this difference in career advancement. The reasons for the fights were because I felt so busy with making my life better by attending college and I resented Kevin for seeming to not care. The bottom line is that I did not respect that he was a hands on man and an entrepreneur by nature. He was motivated by learning as he tried new things. I was motivated by book learning combined with experience. We both just grew to resent the other person's learning style and instead of seeing our spouse's assets we saw only glaring differences that caused us to think that we were totally incompatible. We stopped sharing our experiences with one another because it seemed like neither of us really understood the other.

One way to combat this particular hope buster is to first of all make time for each other especially during the times of change. If you are both pursuing different careers, make the time to check in with each other to see how the other person is enjoying their experience. Just listen and ask questions rather than sharing your opinion of the person's experience. Remember that each of us changes as we get older and what your spouse is now interested in may be different than what you thought they liked, but be an encourager rather then a deterrent to their interest. Confess your thoughts to your spouse about feeling like you are growing apart. Most of us just let these feelings linger and think that they will go away, but unconfessed thoughts that are persistent can create a barrier in your heart towards your spouse that will not allow you to open up before the wall is too big to bring down. Another strategy that may require a sacrifice on your part is to try and take an interest in your spouse's life and changes. For women this is often times easier than it is for men since women are nurturers by nature. Many women will take up fishing, golfing, or hunting for their husbands but it is a rare man who suddenly develops a love for shopping, scrap-booking, cooking, or what many men refer to as "girlie activities". Don't change for your spouse, just do what God calls you to do. Love them unconditionally by knowing them and expressing some interest in their growth as a person. Don't leave the door open for another man or woman to be intrigued or excited about this side of your spouse that is just making you feel more distant from them.

Putting the Kids Before Your Spouse

We spend so much time talking about how many kids we want, pondering pregnancy, and dreaming about that little tiny precious bundle of joy sleeping in our arms that we often forget that having children is a lifetime prospect that changes our reality completely from the inside out. Now there are probably two schools of thought about children, those that say, "We will not allow having kids to change our lives that much. They will work around us and be flexible." Then there are those that live their lives for and around their kids. These are the extremes and there are always those that live somewhere in the middle. Whatever your mindset, bringing children into your life will bring about a shock wave to your couple relationship and it is difficult to understand until you experience it. Education and understanding will at least help prepare you, so if you don't have children don't skip this section. One of the biggest struggles we see with couples is that one of the partners puts the needs of the children before the needs of the spouse. We are not talking about feeding or getting up with a baby. We are talking about an emotional switch that occurs for some parents that put their all into their children and basically turn off towards their spouse. It is a progression that occurs over time, it is not a one–time event. In many ways it is easier to love a child then it is to love a spouse because in their innocent stage children seem easier to love and easier to accept. When your spouse continually disappoints or aggravates you, they do not become more loveable. In fact the opposite dynamic occurs. We become less tolerant of our spouse and less able to understand them. When you have children to project your time and energy into, you can actually be really good at doing this. The digression to putting your kids before your spouse is almost natural, therefore making it all the more dangerous. Children innocently can pit parent against each other by asking mom or dad the same question different times and knowing they will get a different response. Our instinct is to protect our children because they are innocent while our spouse should know better. When it comes to issues of safety this is an absolute truth. Our children should be safe, not abused verbally or physically by our spouse. The issue of discipline should be agreed upon before having children and evaluated throughout the varying lifespan of the child. This is different than the parent that sticks up for their child in every dispute or who tries to protect their child from conflict with the other parent all the time. Or

> *Putting our children above our spouse is a relatively easy trap we can all fall into*

the parent who will bend over backwards to make sure that their child is happy and involved with every sport and activity they need while they haven't taken the time they need to communicate with their spouse or meet their physical needs.

Putting our children above our spouse is a relatively easy trap we can all fall into. Be on the look out for a pattern, a subtle belief in your mind that your children's needs are more important than your spouse's needs. More importantly, take the time with your spouse to ask them to really consider this question "Do I make the children's needs more important than yours? How do I do this? What can I do to change this?" Some of the changes may be possible while others may not be. It is about hearing from your spouse about this. It is also a great idea to talk to a trusted friend that has observed you with your children who can give you honest feedback about what they observe with your behavior towards your children and your spouse.

In the book *The Five Love Languages* by Gary Chapman, he lays out how to understand the way your spouse receives love. It is an easy read and a helpful tool to learn techniques to reach your spouse. It is vitally important to love your spouse in ways that are meaningful to them and different than the ways you meet the needs of your children. This is so difficult especially with large families, because at the end of the day it is exhausting to think of meeting the needs of one more person after you have given your life to your children. There are too many couples that divorce after their children leave the home because they are no longer connected to their spouse. This is often the dangerous combination of putting your life into the children combined with growing apart from your spouse. Having boundaries with our children is the best gift we can give them to teach them about their own emotional regulation and to model to them how a marriage must be nurtured. Most importantly we can leave our children with two intact parents that still love and respect one another and are vitalized, even without children.

Working Too Much

For many men, work means identity and if work is good, then identity is strong. Many wives are also in career fields but our experience has shown us that it is the wives that are hurting because their husbands tend to bury themselves in work. Again, working is essential to being a provider, it says in I Timothy 5:8, *"But if any provide not for his own, and especially for those of his own house, he hath denied the faith and is worse then an infidel."* KJV

Providing for a family is no small task. Unfortunately there has been a blur for many men in providing for a family financially and a deeper understanding of what it means to provide for a wife and children spiritually as a leader in the home. Other words for provider are "supplier, bringer, donor, and source." If you look up comparative words in a thesaurus for "provider" you will find words such as "supporter, promoter and champion." These words are laden with meaning and rife

55

with power. The capacity of a provider to minister to his family is not to be underestimated. Women, you may be the financial provider for the family, but the idea of

> The capacity of a provider to minister to his family is not to be underestimated

working too much will typically not be the temptation of women since they tend to get pulled in many different directions and have to learn to split their time differently to meet the unspoken needs of the family. Again, we are talking about the majority of situations. It is men that will be tempted to put themselves into work and women will put themselves into the children.

Having to work hard as husbands is part of God's original curse to man because of his allowing sin to enter the Garden of Eden, *"because of what you have done, the ground will be under a curse. You will have to work hard all your life to make it to produce enough food for you."* Genesis 3:17 GNB

But make no mistake about it, Jesus became a curse for us so that we do not have to live under this regime. Men can walk in God's original intent for them to commune with Him in the garden while they care for His earth and are good stewards of all that He has blessed them with. There is a balance in not negating the role of the husband to provide while encouraging men to understand how to be a "champion and promoter" to his wife and children. Working too much and being absent from the family interaction can cause many men to become more self–absorbed rather then in tune with what a family may need. The intent here is not to feminize men and make them into pseudo women. It is to empower men to realize that they can set the tone for their home life by being balanced in how much they allow their identity to be set in their work.

It is important for husbands and wives to evaluate the work habits of their family together and make a decision about if there is imbalance in the home and how that is playing out. This is a simple strategy. The bigger issue is for husbands to look at the driving force behind working so much. There are many compelling motivators that cause work to be dominant and some of the ones we have identified are:

Avoiding being at home for various reasons including avoiding conflict, not feeling respected at home, and not feeling like "home is your castle"

- Fear of failure as provider because you grew up in poverty

- Love of money and building a bank account is more of a motivator than being present in home– the tangible results are more meaningful

- Fear of missing professional credibility by appearing lazy

- Debt is higher than income and spending habits of either spouse need to be evaluated

After you evaluate these above motivators, it is important to discuss your priorities as a husband and wife team about what you are both needed in the home for. There are seasons that work must be a priority but if it is a constant source of conflict, then take an honest inventory about if it is a hope buster and change it to the best of your ability. Keep in mind that you will never be on your deathbed and look back and wish you had worked more. Your children will never remember you for the worker you were but for the father or mother you were. They have one example to watch and your habitual choices regarding work, even if well intentioned, to give them a "strong work ethic" may not always produce the desired results if done from the wrong motivation. Later in life, when you tire of work and it is less important to you, the past choices may also have a long–term affect on your spouse's responsiveness towards you.

Sickness / Health Issues

Our vows have the words "in sickness and in health" but most of us probably do not anticipate that sickness will go beyond the mere cold or difficult pregnancy stage. When chronic injury, sickness, or disease is present in marriage it can threaten to wear down both spouses. One of you may be the caregiver and eventually grow to resent your "sick" spouse, while if you are the one who is chronically sick you may grow unrealistically dependent on your spouse for all your needs or you may grow to resent them for being your caregiver.

When you enter the marriage relationship you tend to believe you will do anything for your spouse. However sickness, disease, or hospitalizations can rob you of your desire to nurture and love your spouse because they may be chronic and persistent. There is a loss of dreams when you are dealing with ongoing health issues. You may have been an avid outdoors person and now that is changed in light of your spouse's condition. You may end up quitting a job to stay home and care for a chronically sick husband or wife. Whatever the case, it is easy to fall into a routine rather then actual loving service towards an ailing spouse. The demands of care, the medical bills, and the mood and body changes all associated with sickness, disease, or accidents are draining. There is bound to be guilt from the person needing the care and anger or resentment from the person giving it. Many spouse's blame their partner for the sickness especially if it is related to habits or choices made by the person.

Dealing with sickness or health issues does not have a formulaic response and if we look at Jesus' response to sickness it was always one of compassion followed by healing. He believed always in the wholeness of the person, body, soul, and spirit. The first thing you can do in your marriage if you are sick or dealing with a sick spouse is look to your soul. Take the focus off of the body and focus instead on the inner wounds or healing that need to take place in you. We all know the connection between healing and attitude. The medical journals are replete with this correlation. This is not a new concept it is the original intent of God in creating us. We were formed in HIS image (Genesis 1:26–27). In that respect, we were created perfect. The sickness, diseases, and accidents in this world are the result of living in a fallen world. If we look inward first at our heart, our attitude, and our wounds we can start to find healing for our soul. When our emotions get stronger and our perspective is not marred by previous pain we can start to do all we can to align our bodies with that. If sickness is the result of eating wrong, we can slowly start to change our perspective towards food and perhaps a healthier life will be the result. If we have relied on pain pills to deal with chronic issues in our body, with a renewed mind and soul perhaps we will find other means to deal with chronic pain. This is not a quick fix or one size fits all approach. Some diseases and sicknesses never go away. Again if we look to our soul and our mind first we can be renewed and healed to approach even chronic sickness from a spiritual perspective.

> *If we look inward first at our heart, our attitude, and our wounds we can start to find healing for our soul*

Another strategy in dealing with sickness and disease is to acknowledge the burden; both of carrying the sickness, disease, or injury; and caring for the person with it. We are always afraid of hurting our spouse but we must learn to speak the truth, if not speaking it is causing resentment or hurt to brew. The key is to follow the example of Jesus when he tells us in John 8:32 *"You shall know the truth and the truth shall set you free."* NKJV

Again, the key is speaking the truth in love with the goal to restore and bring healing (See Ephesians 4:15). You can tell your spouse lovingly, "I need a break, I love you but I don't want to get worn out so I am taking some time to get refreshed." Time to refuel is critical when caring for a sick spouse and time for them to connect with another person with a fresh perspective is also critical. Each of you is carrying a very distinct burden and it is imperative to connect as married persons rather then patient and caregiver. Tell your sick spouse what they give you emotionally, physically, and spiritually; acknowledge their contribution to your life. In the same vein it is critical that the caregiver not just be acknowledged for their care giving ability but for their other characteristics as a spouse. Using respite care if necessary is also vital to reenergize both of you for the continued road ahead of you.

Most importantly be aware at all times of what it is you are feeling. Do not live by your feelings but if you continue to have feelings of anger, resentment, depression, or loss continually then it is a sign that you may need some support or prayer or even a new perspective. Much of perspective is found in taking a short break, change of scenery, acknowledging truth, and looking at what hurts still need healing inside of you. Sometimes just holding one another close, asking God to equip you for your situation, and acknowledging that there is nothing you can do is enough to release your stress. Lastly, never forget that our God is Jehovah Rapha the Healer. In Isaiah 53, he tells us that it is *"by His stripes that we are healed."* We can acknowledge that truth even while sickness is present in our body. It is not a contradiction. It is God's truth and we are still acknowledging His sovereignty even when we do not understand why sickness is present in our body or the body of our spouse. The key is in understanding that sin is present in this world, there is disease, corruption, defilement and sickness, and God isn't randomly handing out death sentences to some and life to others. We must look to His original design for us and strive to be perfected inwardly even if our body seems to be wasting away.

Lack of Intimacy and Sexual Dissatisfaction

Why is it we are compelled by that sexual attraction so much prior to marriage and then many marriages are void of a sexual relationship after the marriage? Lack of sexual intimacy is a major issue for many couples especially after marriage. The usual enemies of this are time and busyness, other distractions like pornography, the shame of sex before marriage, physical changes, losing attraction to your spouse, and just finding that sex is not that satisfying. There are of course other factors but these are the main ones that we have found when working with couples. Since sex is the closest you can get to another person physically, the act of sex has a lot of power. If you have body issues and shame issues, sex may become burdensome and even embarrassing. If you feel your spouse doesn't find you attractive you may want to get it

> *Lack of sexual intimacy is a major issue for many couples especially after marriage*

over with. One of you may be more sexually needy than the other and that can get tiring fighting over that.

Every situation is different but for the most part it is men that are attracted visually and therefore may want to engage in sex more than the wife due to being physically stimulated. Wives may complain about this and often the husband may begin to feel like he is a burden. Or conversely the husband may be engaging in pornography and may have a visual image of the perfect sexual partner and may be more and more dissatisfied with his wife. And then there are the hormonal and physical changes that accompany pregnancy, childbearing, and post pregnancy that make it difficult to have an enjoyable sex life.

Talk About It

Whatever your situation is regarding sex, the first thing you must do is talk about it. This may sound easy to say but because the sexual relationship has been so stigmatized and made dirty in the church many people feel it is best to keep these matters quiet. Of course we are not advocating for public forums to discuss your sexual problems. We are advocating first talking to one another. Marriage is the deepest form of intimacy so therefore talking about our sexual relationship should be a natural part of our conversation. Set aside some time to talk about these matters if it is too awkward to talk about it when you are in the middle of trying to get intimate. Lay out the issue clearly, "I feel embarrassed about my body when I'm with you so I'm not very expressive and want to get it over with," or "I have lost interest in sex lately and it is not you, you are attractive to me. I'm wondering what is going on with me physically or emotionally because I'd like to be intimate more." Coming in with a plan to discuss the situation makes it a lot less threatening for the spouse that has to receive the information.

If there are bigger factors at play like pornography or even lustful thoughts towards someone else, these are issues that need intervention or strategies from outside help (see addiction or adultery section). If there are deeper issues like sexual abuse that have made you more cautious about your sexual relationship or your body, it is important to start with yourself. Seek Godly counsel to find healing and explore how you view sex. Some questions to consider as a starting point may be:

- How has sex been modeled in your life?

- What was your role and what was expected of you?

- How did your family of origin express sex or sexual ideas and nudity?

- Do you understand boundaries and what they mean for sexual or body issues?

Working these issues through in a sexual abuse survivor group or through prayer and ministry with a trusted same–sex pastor or counselor may relieve the fear, tension, and lack of trust or interest you bring to the sexual partnership.

Again if you are in a trusting marriage relationship that has bumps like any other you can really glean a lot from just being honest with your spouse and sharing hurts, ambiguity, or confusion with them. Just the intimate act of your spouse knowing your fears can break you through to a deeper level of intimacy. Being able to pray over one another about insecurities and shame related to sex is another healing tool.

Another big factor to consider in your relationship is how you view your spouse's sexual relationships prior to marriage. The knowledge of that alone can be a distraction and a deterrent for many people to feel truly connected with their spouse. This makes sense from a biblical perspective. From the beginning of creation in Genesis after Eve had sinned, the one thing she and Adam became aware of was their nakedness (See Genesis 3:7). They were ashamed. Sin makes us aware of our bodies, our flaws, and our imperfections. Nudity is raw and exposed and therefore without God's blessing we are inclined to cover it. We also learn to cover sexual sins, not by using fig leaves like Adam and Eve, but by lying to our spouse about our sexual temptations, or about covering up what was done to us sexually, or by not communicating about our sexual needs to our spouse. These are all cover-ups in the sexual arena and they are the "natural" inclination of our fallen self. The Genesis account amplifies our need for close communion with God and the bleak exposure we experience when we choose sin rather than His protection.

I Corinthians 6:18–19 tells us *"run away from sexual sin. No other sin so clearly affects the body as this one does. For sexual immorality is a sin against your own body. Or don't you know that your body is a temple of the Holy Spirit who lives in you and was given to you by God. You do not belong to yourself."* NLT

When we experience a sexual relationship outside of the marriage covenant whether before marriage with random people, or with our future spouse, we are affected. The body houses your mind and your emotions so it makes sense that those aspects of yourself would be tied into the sexual experience with your spouse as well. You may be inclined to think about a previous sexual encounter you have had while trying to focus on your current married

> *God does allow us to have second chances and He desires to take shame out of the sexual relationship*

sexual relationship. Or you may also fantasize about how great the sex was between you and your spouse prior to marriage. This is why it is so critical to treat your body as the temple that God tells you it is.

Kevin and I used to think that all those rules in church about not having sex before marriage were old and outdated and definitely not for advanced people like us. We learned very quickly through our own choices and through listening to others experiences that these ideas were God's ideas. Why? Because He knew beforehand that our entire being; our bodies, minds, and hearts would be clearly affected by the sexual experience.

This is why we must really consider our actions with our spouse prior to marriage and understand the deep implications the sexual choice can have on our marriage later on.

Ask for forgiveness from your spouse and pray with them if you can about allowing yourself to sin against your own body with another or with your spouse prior to marriage. God does allow us to have second chances and He desires to take shame out of the sexual relationship and give us the opportunity to experience intimacy at a deeper level with our spouse than we had. The first step is bringing truth to the relationship and gaining God's perspective on it, then evaluating if there is a need to involve a third party in the conversation, and lastly to keep open dialogue with your spouse about sex and sexual dimensions of yourself. Obliterating shame, and hurt over sexual issues is critical to a new beginning. Sex really can be a way to connect with your spouse, meet their needs fairly easily, and keep you in tune to one another. Sometimes, it is as simple as just making the choice to connect sexually and allow God to work even when you don't feel like it means anything to you.

Taking it Home

1. Are there any of the above hope busters that you can identify as being a contributor to the loss of hope in your marriage? In what way?

2. What does the loss of hope look like to you in your marriage? I.E. What does your spouse say or do that could cause feelings of hopelessness? Be specific.

3. What could your spouse do to help increase hope in your marriage? Action or word? What could you do? Action or word?

HOPE CHALLENGE

You know those things that make your spouse smile–chocolate chip cookies, coffee, a card, prayer, being held, a movie, eye contact, saying you are sorry. Choose two to do this week for your spouse, don't tell them. Just bless them and watch hope grow.

Chapter 3 – Identifying and Dealing with Hope Busters – Part II

Financial Strain

"For the love of money is a root of all kinds of evil, for which some have strayed from the faith in their greediness, and pierced themselves through with many sorrows." I Timothy 6:10 NKJV

We have all heard this and it probably elicits a different response in each of us depending on your experience with money. There are two typical life experiences with money,

1.) You had enough and were taken care of, or

2.) You never had enough.

These very different perspectives cause our relationship with money to look different. When we get married we are marrying two philosophies about money. Now of course none of us would admit that we love money, the distinction Jesus was making is clear– money or having it is not inherently wrong, the point is our attitude towards money.

When you and your spouse approach financial decisions in the early years it can be a source of adventure and fun as you decide how and what to spend your money on. However as you continue in your marriage and in making financial decisions together there can be strain as you differ on how to spend your money. Questions arise like how much is appropriate to spend on hobbies? Eating out? Vacations? Shopping? Or whatever it is that you are interested in. It is a precarious balance to manage money in this economy, let alone balance the two spending habits of very different people.

Many issues arise like overspending, hoarding money, credit card debt, and anger over how a spouse spends money, and pressure mounts on how to differ want from need. At the heart of many of these issues is our family of origin experience. Sometimes we may react from a poverty mentality and not expect to live life with any financial benefits, or other times we may enter the marriage with an entitlement perspective because we are used to being taken care of financially. This is somewhat oversimplifying it but the bottom line is that money issues cause more conflict than many of the other hope busters combined.

Money, or having it is not inherently wrong, the point is our attitude towards money

The surest and best way to understand the financial differences between you and your spouse is by having a budget even before you get married. This starts with conversation about how you like to spend money. Evaluate yourself first; are you quick to spend money even when it is not in the budget? Other questions to ask could be:

- What is your attitude towards credit?

- Are you cautious and scared to spend money because of how you grew up and so you hoard it and never allow your spouse and yourself to indulge?

- Does one of you eat out more?

- Does one of you like shopping for clothes more?

- What about hobbies? How is the money dispersed for hobbies?

It helps to have an agreement about what amount of money you and your spouse can spend without consulting each other. Sit down and actually look at how each of you spends money. These are critical areas to evaluate together and they are also areas that can cause tension, so preparation in your heart and in your mind is critical prior to having that conversation.

Have an Eternal Perspective

Perhaps the most important thing you and your spouse can agree on is what is the purpose of money? If you can both get a Godly perspective on wealth such as *"The earth is the Lords and all its fullness."* Psalm 24:1 NKJV

It can free you from the bondage many people feel about finances. If it is God Himself that has given you the power to get wealth and the ability to work to obtain that wealth then surely He needs to be part of the equation of how and where you choose to spend your money. Making sure you have that eternal perspective on money will allow you the freedom to not let money have control over you. This is a very difficult paradigm to obtain because we live in a world that stresses credit scores, house size, furniture, type of car, vacations taken, and size of financial portfolio. While arguably all these things make life simpler, easier, and more comfortable, they are not a measure of a person's true self. Evaluate your perspective on the world system of financial success and diligently seek God to show you how HE would have you manage your finances.

The biggest issue in any marriage is to look at the hold money has on you. It is not always the obvious ways. Just because you don't spend much money doesn't mean you are not controlled by money. Your fear of losing money or not having enough is an indicator that money is a stronghold for you and a barrier to freedom in Christ. Identify this belief system if you have it and recognize where the root came from; was it the childhood of food stamps? The

> *It is imperative to honor God with the first fruits of all your increase through tithing*

fighting the parents always did about having no money? Was it the fear you felt when your dad lost his job or when you saw mom crying over the bills? Lack of financial resources in childhood can be a mortifying and heavy weight but it does not need to propel you into a future where you either respond by taking control of your own finances out of fear, or you yourself lose control of finances out of helplessness. There can be balance by taking on God's perspective. *"And my God shall supply all your need according to HIS riches in Glory by Christ Jesus."* Philippians4:19 NKJV

God knows what you need before you ask and when the economy fails and it becomes harder and harder to see the results of your hard work, you can trust in God that He will not let you down even if your checkbook is in the negative balance.

During these times of trial or even differences in how you and your spouse spend money it is imperative to honor God with the first fruits of all your increase through tithing (See Proverbs 3:9). Do your best to pay your bills and be honorable by not overspending and communicating with all those that you owe money to. If you are in a reverse situation where you feel your spouse has such a reign and control on money then you can only pray for their perspective to become eternally based and continue to approach them on ways you would like to spend the money. Allow God to release the finances in due season. Give as you can and put your security in God, not your checkbook. Do not resent your spouse for this stronghold in their life. Overall the best financial strategy is preventative– stop the overspending before you get there by recognizing and limiting your spending habits. Agree on money spent for hobbies and fun. Lastly, give generously to your church and to others that you know can use the blessing. Giving to others releases you from the grip of money. Money is just the secular medium of exchange for services rendered, it is man created and must be regulated in a Godly manner.

Physical Abuse/Emotional Abuse

Abuse is, perhaps, one of the hardest issues to confront in the church; especially when many times the scriptures from Ephesians 5 about submission have been so misconstrued that many women have felt they must submit to a tyrant with no hope of escape. Being beaten down verbally and physically can rob you of all hope quicker then most things can. Losing your identity at the hands, or by the words, of the person you consider your intimate partner is defiling and humiliating at the very least.

So what is abuse then? With the feminist movement we see an emasculating of the very nature of men, in that if they are passionate or bold in any way then women cry oppression or abuse. Conversely with the culture of the early 1900's, we see an acceptance of harshness from men to women as commonplace. A woman must be kept in her place and whatever it took to put her there is all right as long as she submits to the man. Both views misconstrue God's original intent and design for the husband/wife relationship.

Gods View On Marriage Helps Us Understand Abuse

There are factors that contribute to abuse in a relationship that must be understood before you can even begin to build a marriage on a sure foundation. The research is replete with statistics on abuse. However one thing is not always agreed upon, what is abuse exactly? Many define it as just the words that hurt you, or even the environment that is uncomfortable for you. Whatever your frame of reference, your upbringing, and your own security level in your communication; this will impact how you define abuse. A proper view of God's intent for marriage is essential for you to look at your relationship and know if there is abuse there.

Ephesians 5 gives us very clear direction about the individual roles that each spouse should accept in marriage. The entire chapter is an exhortation to the church at Ephesus about walking in love. The premise is defining what love will look like when walked out in relationship, one of those relationships being the marriage.

The first key in understanding this love walk is to see that we are called to be "children of light" (Ephesians 5:8). If you or your spouse do not understand the truth of a relationship with Jesus Christ then a relationship free of abuse may not always be possible especially if there are predisposing factors

> *The first key in understanding this love walk is to see that we are called to be "children of light"*

that make you more prone to being attracted to abusive people or being abusive or controlling yourself. This book will not go into what all those factors are but it is important to understand the childhood and family of origin components that are linked to abuse. So if we say we are children of light, we get married, and we cannot properly walk in love and find ourselves using words and actions that consistently bring death to our spouse, then we must look deeper.

We're told in verses 21–30 of Ephesians 5 that there is a rhythm that our marriage can take when we are properly submitted to Christ. We are each given a distinct role to follow. For wives it is to understand that the husband is the head or as we like to put it, "the last say," and for husbands it is to love her even unto death. Again, if we view this in context we are both committed to walking in love as children of light. Then we can have the expectation that our spouse understands their respective roles and we don't have to be responsible for their fulfilling of it. If however, a husband is falling short of loving his wife as Christ loved the church, and is exercising his own authority rather than an authority grounded in his relationship with Christ, then his behavior must be scrutinized on that merit. A man who simply keeps his wife down through oppression, unkind words, physical restraint, or intimidation is not walking in love. As a wife we are not called to submit to that behavior, our first and foremost call is to submit to God. Our body is His temple, our behavior should reflect His love and we can respectfully and lovingly resist evil done upon us. Remember in verse 24 it tells us, *"Now as the church submits to Christ, so also wives should submit to their husbands in everything."* NKJV

If you break that verse down then you as a wife are being asked to submit to the husband as the church submits to Christ. Christ does not ask the church body to submit to His oppression, control, or abuse. He freely gives us a choice to "come unto Him" as "He knocks at the door of our heart". Our willingness to obey and submit to Christ as His church is based on our relationship with HIM founded on love and His gentle leadership.

Take Sole Responsibility for Your Behavior

Take the time to evaluate your behavior towards your spouse; is it one of submission and love for Christ? If not then you can identify that there may be work for you to do in regards to your conversation and words or physical actions to your spouse. If there is blatant physical harm being done in a marriage, this is not love, this is not an action that God condones to bring unity to the marriage. It doesn't mean that God cannot deliver you from this stronghold of anger, emotional control, rage, or even abusive words or behavior. It is, however, a process by which the person inflicting these wounds must take sole responsibility for their actions and seek help. The other party has a responsibility still to be reverent towards Christ, to walk in love and to evaluate their own wounds and seek help. Abuse will not ever provide an environment for healing or hope. Once the person identifies their habits, patterns, and actions and seeks help then hope can come; but only if the commitment to seek accountability and submission to being a child of light is done.

Many marriages have had to separate while they were seeking guidance and help for abuse in their relationship. The key factor is safety, especially with children and knowing that you are both committed to being more like Christ. Then a wife's submission is based on her husband's pursuit to lead her, not his pursuit to dominate or rule over her in control. A husband must be willing to lead by example, but also know that when it comes to leading he is the general and she is the private so to speak. He has much responsibility for his wife and abuse will never achieve results. Since submission is actually a military word

> *Christ cares for the church. He feeds them and clothes them by providing a relationship with Him and teaching us through His example and His word*

that means "obey, be under, be in subjection." It is only used correctly by a wife submitting to a man that is "in God" and that "loves his wife as Christ loves the church"(vs. 25). He is Christ like and in being like this he should not be abusive. If he is, then help must be sought.

Strategies in Dealing With Abuse

There are many anger management groups available to deal with the problem of abuse or control. If the problem of abuse–emotionally or physically –in your relationship is not getting better then it may be time to look at a group. These groups are typically designed for personal responsibility and teaching about anger, triggers, recognizing thoughts, and even family of origin factors contributing to the choices to act abusively. It is imperative that each person seeks individual help before coming together to "solve" the marriage problem. Since we are specifically told in God's word that we each have respective roles in the marriage then it makes sense, that in order to learn more about those roles and seek help for our failures in fulfilling them, that we would look at ourselves individually before seeking help as a couple.

As Ephesians 5:29 tells us *"after all, no one ever hated his own body, but he feeds and cares for it, just as Christ does the church."* NKJV

The word of God is clear, we have a responsibility to take care of our body, to feed ourselves with food that helps us grow, not only in a physical sense, but also in a spiritual and emotional sense. Christ cares for the church. He feeds them and clothes them by providing a relationship with Him and teaching us through His example and His word. So we ought to do all that we can to leave that legacy of love for our spouse. Being honest about our behaviors, actions, and attitudes is a step to do this.

Kevin and I had abuse in our relationship. How did we know that? The environment was hostile and controlling and both of us, at varying times, were trying to make a point through intimidation or oppression. That's how we knew. Kevin was very rageful, not just towards me but towards inanimate objects. His anger and ranting created a home environment where we felt like we were walking on eggshells. He used lots of excuses for it. He was too tired, nothing worked like it should, not enough money or similar. Whatever the excuse, I just thought this was normal. There was anger, rage, ranting, swearing and tension.

I responded in kind by letting this wall of hurt build up. This hurt turned to hate and ultimately I responded in kind by throwing plants, plates, or whatever I could get my hands on to be stronger, and more intimidating than him. This is also the time when I learned to use the control of the silent treatment. I knew if I left him without telling him where I was going then I had the upper hand and it hurt him deeply. This was a very painful chapter in our lives, a period where we left such a poor legacy and example for our son, a period that brought much shame. Who wants to admit they are out of control? Who wants to tell a fellow believer or friend that they screamed or swore or threw something? There was not a place to be honest, so the secret brewed between us. Eventually the anger, rage and pain contributed to the breakdown and our eventual divorce.

Abuse creates an environment of strife and self-loathing. When there is strife, there is such a loss of hope and when there is self loathing there is shame. These factors combine to make it more difficult to seek the help you really need. One person has to be strong enough to make the first move. If you abuse by words or actions, admit it to a trusted friend and get help and accountability through counseling or through a group. If you are hiding behind a wall of shame because of your home environment, then seek help, set the standard, and ask God to allow the healing you need to come. You are not helping a person fulfill their God given role by allowing their anger to flourish and dominate your home life. When Kevin and I committed to remarriage we had to seek individual counsel and commit to an environment of total honesty about our actions and behaviors that were destructive and painful. This coupled with a commitment to church attendance, and surrounding ourselves with those friends we knew would hold us accountable allowed us to remarry with a renewed purpose of having a relationship free of abuse or control. A relationship that was free to feel hopeful again.

Addictions

When your spouse turns his or her affections to another person it crushes and betrays you, but when their attention is turned to a substance or a habit it can really perplex and burden you in uncommon ways. Addiction is also described in words like "compulsion", "dependence", "need", "craving" or "infatuation" (New Oxford American Dictionary). There are so many things that vie for our time in this world, and unfortunately for many of us they can turn into addictions. Evaluate the other words for addiction and see what behaviors, choices, or habits you may engage in that fit into that category.

The most common forms of addiction are alcohol, tobacco use, drugs (prescription or illegal), sex, pornography, work, gambling, exercise or eating, and spending money (shopping, online etc). Of course there are other caveats that fit into any one of these categories as well. The thing to look at is where do you spend most of your time or energy. If you are thinking about the activity or craving it or feeling like you need it to relax, then it is time to evaluate yourself more deeply. Romans 12:1 exhorts us, *"give your bodies to God. Let them be a living and Holy sacrifice–the kind He will accept."* NLT

How many times have we given ourselves halfheartedly to God because we are distracted or influenced by an addiction of some kind. It is impossible inasmuch as we give ourselves to our addiction to give our authentic self to God or our spouse completely. It is difficult to pay attention fully to the other person's pain or needs if we are distracted by our own cravings.

I encourage you to evaluate what it is your soul is craving. You can do this by first of all discerning what you spend the most time thinking about. Are you distracted with plans you may be making to engage in your habit or addiction? Is your mind numb, or conversely, too full to really hear your spouse or be interested in them? In Romans 12, the Word goes on to

> *We must include God in the internal dialogue we are having with ourselves when the addiction is knocking on our door*

encourage us to, *"let God transform you into a new person by changing the way you think."*

This takes deliberate steps on your part including giving yourself new things to focus on or think about. Memorize scripture, pray out loud, learn a language, get busy with exercise, or read a book. These are many activities that can shift the focus of your thoughts. The word of God goes even deeper than telling us to divert or shifting thoughts, it tells us not to be conformed to the customs of this world but to be transformed in our minds by God. How do we do that?

We must include God in the internal dialogue we are having with ourselves when the addiction is knocking on our door. I dare you to invite God into that part of your thought process. Interrupt it by saying a loud, "Why am I thinking this way?" or "I ask you Lord to help me right now in Jesus' name. I can't do this alone." Or even better, calling and admitting that thought to a friend, or trusted prayer partner. Hearing the thought in words helps you break it down for what it is and evaluate what is or is not truth. Interjecting God's truth into your thought process begins with first recognizing that God is sovereign anyway.

> *The second strategy is to listen to what it is you talk about.*

He is all knowing and knows what you are struggling with but you must move toward Him, not away from Him. Make a choice to verbalize His presence in your thought process. It is a first step towards seeking help for the addiction.

The second strategy is to listen to what it is you talk about. Do you talk excessively about work? About your weight or diet? Do you find yourself talking about your plans as they relate to your next "fix", or "work project", or "shopping outing"? What you are saying is more than likely what you are really about.

Luke 6:45b states *"For of the abundance of the heart his mouth speaketh."* NLT

This is talking about the connection between our mouth and our heart, what we have in our deepest longings usually proceeds to come out of our mouth at some time. Just listen to what you are talking about and then you know that you have just jumped from thinking about addictive behaviors, to talking or focusing on it, you are one step away from doing it. The obvious strategy is to stop talking about it, stop confessing the hold it has on you, and start confessing the new belief system or lifestyle you are pursuing. If you are struggling with overeating, it begins with the thought process. But if you say, "I'm hungry," or "I need chocolate," you've already fueled the thought by words. Friend, action is right at the heels of spoken word. Changing the way we communicate is one of the hardest parts of our human walk simply because there are nuances, or habitual ways of relating that we become all too familiar with. If there are ritualistic ways you talk about your addiction recognize them and confess them to someone trusted and change the language you use to relate to this aspect of your life. If you have never talked about the addiction and you have only kept it inward, then just learning to talk about it honestly will be a first step in understanding what is actually in your heart. Keeping your thoughts hidden from the world when they lead to addictive behavior is the surest way to continue in addiction.

Lastly, with any addiction or compulsion, after recognizing the loss or need that fuels the beginning of the thought process and then changing the way you talk; it is important to confess the sin to a Godly person and then evaluate a way to involve your spouse in the recovery process. Getting free from addiction to pain meds may feel like an individual recovery process but it is a marital problem because it has been affecting the way you have related in your marriage. You can't just suddenly decide that the money you've been slowly sneaking out of the bank account to feed your gambling addiction is irrelevant to your spouse.

You Can't Do It Alone

Often we try to tackle addictive behaviors and sins alone without our spouse for a variety of reasons; namely we don't want to get preached at or ragged on, we don't want to hurt them, we are embarrassed by our choices, or we believe we can handle it on our own. These approaches all run contrary to God's plan for marriage. The covenant itself is sacred between husband and wife and if you are one after marriage then you can be sure that your behaviors and choices, even if unknown to your spouse, have affected them in significant ways.

There must be truth in the relationship for there to be wholeness.

Christ died for us and all of our sins. He says if we confess our sins He is faithful and just to forgive us our sins. Confession is a big part of any recovery and allowing your spouse to confront their own fears about your addiction will also allow them to grow. This last strategy may involve seeking help, treatment, or counseling that is fueled by truth and setting you free rather than keeping you in the addictive mindset. Look into help that will involve your spouse at some level. Some situations may require third party intervention, while others may not. Whatever your case, remember that you are not made to carry burdens alone. That is why you have been given a spouse. Your daily load is your responsibility but if your addictive or compulsive behaviors have been eroding your marriage, bring the burden to another for Godly counsel and help.

Infidelity / Adultery

We saved this particular hope buster for last not because it is the worst, but because it is the most complex. Other words for infidelity and adultery are "falseness," "treachery," "betrayal," "deceitfulness," and "unfaithfulness." Strong words are used to explain intense actions; therefore the affect of adultery on

> The wrong choices are multifaceted and include the choices of both spouses not just the "betrayer"

a marriage cannot be oversimplified. Many people who have experienced adultery either as the "adulterer" or the "victim of adultery" would tell you that there is no way they would have ever seen themselves in this situation. It is critical that we understand that each of these hope buster behaviors originate with thoughts, these thoughts lead to choices, these choices than may lead to hurtful behavior. Adultery is the culmination of a series of wrong choices that opened a door to the ultimate act of betrayal.

The wrong choices are multifaceted and include the choices of both spouses not just the "betrayer". This is a difficult pill for many spouses to swallow, but it is the painful truth. The definitive choice to betray belongs solely to the person who chose adultery as the outlet and expression for their pain, but it is critical to analyze the couple dynamic to look for the open doors and the gaps in the relationship that need to be filled. This is not to say that a spouse can fulfill all your needs and that if a marriage is done right then there will never be room for adultery. That is unrealistic. It is looking at the "truthfulness" and "intimacy" of the marriage relationship to evaluate if the marriage itself is an honest mirror of Christ's love being demonstrated between two people. This is a messy process and if adultery has occurred it is a painful time to do this because the wounds are very deep.

88

What Is Adultery?

Let us first define for you what infidelity and adultery are. We looked at similar words to understand the breadth and depth of the meaning of adultery, but now let's look at the nuts and bolts of these actions. The first question we as outsiders always want to know about affairs is if the two people had sexual relations. This is because the sexual act is the ultimate expression of connection so we assume that is the best definition of adultery. It is only a part of it. The deeper way to understand infidelity is to look at the meaning of the word. If falseness is part of infidelity then any action with a person other then your spouse that causes you to have a false response with your spouse; is infidelity.

Let's break it down. If you are having conversations with another person of the opposite sex at work, or anywhere else, that you need to keep from your spouse, you need to consider those actions and what they may be opening the door to. If you are in a place where you are "false" or not representing truth to your spouse because you are worried about their reaction or hurting them, then you are in danger. You may be saying "there is no way I would ever have sex with another person" or "there is no way I would ever let it get that far." These good intentions must be backed by the corresponding behavior. Looking at this meaning even deeper let's say you have a neglectful, spouse who is very uninterested in a sexual relationship with you suddenly, and you find yourself in a situation where you are in the wrong place at the wrong time and you "fall into a one time sexual relationship" with someone. You brush it under the rug justifying it as a slip or a bad decision. You decide not to tell your spouse because it will hurt them. This experience makes you look like the passive, defenseless bystander in your life but it does not negate your choice to allow your defenses to weaken to the point where you put yourself in vulnerable situations. These two experiences are vastly different but both are representations of the varying expressions of adultery and infidelity.

There are many other variations of the two examples above that include the long–term affair that started as a friendship, led to deep emotional intimacy, and then led to the physical relationship. Now there is a deep adulterous relationship going on between two adults that believe they are in love with one another. Some of these relationships start because the original marriage was in a weak spot or because of choices to carry a friendship further than friends. The crucial decision in these cases is whether or not the adulterous relationship will lead to a break up of the marriage or marriages involved and if the couple will try to stay together.

There are other relationships that may include maintaining a close friendship with a person from your past that you still have feelings for and using them for support in the difficult times of your life. We used the example above of the one time sexual relationship; these often lead to multiple one–night stands. The guilt is oppressive for a short time but it is short lived until the next time it happens. Eventually the cumulative affect of one–night stands is self–loathing, lack of intimacy between you and your spouse, and a guilty defensive reaction to your spouse. In between all of these are the internet relationships that we say are nothing but we are using to garner emotional support, or the "special" flirtatious friendship we continue to maintain because it is innocent but fun.

Understanding adultery and infidelity takes a heart willing to look into the darkest place of our own humanity and capacity for sin and shine the light of truth and compassion. It is not easy to do because our need and our drive for connection is sometimes much stronger than our need and our desire to be whole and complete. If we are in the affair, we like the feelings it elicits in us and begin to believe that those feelings are very real. We withdraw from marriage and often are convinced that we married the wrong person. Again, because our spouse rubs us the wrong way or cause us to feel sadness, loneliness, or other feelings, we believe this other person can complete us. The adulterous relationship is a place where we feel fulfilled, connected, and needed; the opposite of what we experience in our marriage.

To understand how this progression of thoughts to extremely hurtful behavior happens, we must first be willing to admit that the primary purpose of marriage is not to make us happy. That is not a novel concept in a culture of self–determinism and self–gratification. We often state, "I deserve to be happy." But our instruction on marriage found in Ephesians 5 and Colossians 3 are very clear that we have our respective role to accomplish in marriage. These roles are about demonstrating unconditional love and respect to our spouse. There is not a section in these portions of scripture about pursuing our own individual happiness or good feelings.

However, the result of both people pouring of themselves into one another produces a reciprocal growing relationship, of which happiness is easily a byproduct. This is of course dependent on both parties doing their part and we all know this is not consistent 100% of the time during a marriage. More then likely

> *Adultery is just another demonstration of the depth of our depravity*

marriage growth ebbs and flows and there are times when one gives and one takes and circumstances affect your ability to give completely of yourself to your spouse. These difficult circumstances are the times when we may weaken in our commitment and the doors are opened to allow thoughts of adultery or infidelity to enter. These are also the times when we start to entertain thoughts about how unhappy we are and how happy that other person makes us feel. It takes a deep understanding of our own weakness coupled with a heart of compassion to grasp that we all possess the capacity towards sin. Adultery is just another demonstration of the depth of our depravity. Once we comprehend this about ourselves, and then understand the hurts within our spouse, we may then begin to forgive an adulterous spouse.

Unmet Needs Open the Door to Adultery

There is no justification for the choice of adultery in any form. The key is truth about the adultery and uncovering the open doors in the relationship that make it vulnerable to this sin. More than likely the person who commits adultery has an unmet need. If you can start by tracing that need back to its origin then you can see that more than likely it did not originate in the marriage. If you begin to feel controlled by your wife in your marriage it is more than likely you had a controlling parent, probably a mother. When you married that person you loved their decisiveness, their independence, but through the course of the marriage you are reminded of how controlling that person seems and how you feel controlled. Then some other demure young lady starts to notice you, you converse, and suddenly you feel respected, not controlled. Thus the very benign cycle begins. You are seeking to feel less controlled because you have been controlled your whole life but have never dealt with the original source of your feelings; your mother. Now your wife is the target of your hurt, frustration, and withdrawal. You feel like you have told her over and over again and she doesn't change. She still controls you so you withdraw and now you are in a relationship with another woman. Now it is a perfect set up for your wife to be perceived as even more and more controlling because you feel so free finally. She keeps nagging you and making demands of you. The outcome: it pushes you further away from her and into the arms of the other woman.

Another helpful strategy in identifying the path that opened various emotional doors to an adulterous relationship is to write out a timeline of when negative thought patterns have entered your relationship and how you responded to them as time went on. What was the relationship like with your spouse when these thoughts or patterns emerged? Was it during a time of intense change? Trauma? Loss? Typically we can identify a guiding thought pattern that starts out somewhat innocent like, "He never listens to me" or "She doesn't really respect me." These thoughts are connected to negative experiences or unresolved conflicts with our spouse and through time they build up as they are unanswered or if your needs continue to be unmet. Whether you are the one who committed adultery or the one that was the victim of adultery this is a helpful strategy to identify the breakdown in your unity and intimacy with your spouse. The timeline can be used with your spouse as you journey down the path of rebuilding by uncovering ways you both respond and react to pain and conflict in the relationship.

> *There is no one–time strategy that is foolproof in rebuilding a marriage after adultery*

Boundaries Help

Another important tool is to recognize your boundaries or lack of boundaries with people of the opposite sex. Do you find yourself having intimate lunches with a trusted friend of the opposite sex? Do you find yourself working late with someone of the opposite sex because it is fulfilling and you don't want to go home and face life there? We all have different weaknesses in this area and some of us are more prone to being vulnerable with people of the opposite sex. Find a trusted friend who you can be accountable to about your own personal boundaries and also a friend that you can run scenarios by which involve you and another person of the opposite sex. Building hedges around your personal life is frowned upon in this culture but if you have allowed yourself to be vulnerable in this area, it is the only way to build trust again with your spouse and to hold yourself accountable as well.

There is no one–time strategy that is foolproof in rebuilding a marriage after adultery. There are layers to uncover and the rebuilding process can be very painful and sometime hurt more than the revelation of adultery itself. Our typical response to adultery is shock and then we respond with varying degrees of anger that can lead to unforgiveness or bitterness and possibly divorce. There is also the more subtle response of progressive denial that many couples enter into in order to save face, save the marriage, forgive and forget, or protect their children from the pain of this betrayal. Either of these two responses are not long lasting and are not indicative of true repentance and true reconciliation.

What is Reconciliation?

The Greek word for reconciliation means to "change thoroughly" or to "change mutually." A thorough change indicates that it is throughout the entire person and thus it will affect the person's entire world especially the inner workings of their marriage. You cannot choose to be reconciled to your spouse after an adulterous relationship without there being evidence of change. Many of us that have experienced adultery, either by committing it or having it committed against us, say we don't have to prove anything to anyone that God forgives and that is all there is to it. True, God does forgive us completely but if we are to walk out His forgiveness in the true Biblical spirit of reconciliation, that change must be evident. It will mean that our comfortable ways of communicating, our familiar patterns of withdrawing, defensiveness, yelling, silence, or intellectualizing must be challenged until we see real change within ourselves and within our interactions with our spouse. It also means that we will have to change our relationship with the person we committed adultery with. We will have to cut that relationship off to truly reconcile with our spouse.

We cannot get weary that our spouse may need to process pain or have trouble forgiving and trusting us. At the same time we cannot just choose to hold the adultery over our spouse's head for the rest of our married relationship causing them to feel like they "owe us one" because of what they did to us. There is a precarious and delicate dance we must engage in to be purposeful in putting the memory of the wound out of our minds but also being mindful that an appropriate amount of processing, and mutual discussion, is vital to rebuilding trust again.

We may feel like we are so sick of proving to the world that we have changed or proving to our spouse that we are trustworthy once again. That is why we need this change to be something that only God can do. It is through seeking His presence in our life and focusing on our relationship with Him that we will find ourselves transformed. We cannot create change by acting better; we must also wait patiently for our minds and emotions to respond to this new pattern of reconciliation.

Walk It Out

The biggest issue is to just walk out the changes no matter how false they feel. With Kevin and me it was learning to talk about our pain in a more real way when Kevin felt like I was disrespecting him or comparing him to the person I was in relationship with. During these times it was hard for him to see me as loveable, so he just told me that. Sometimes he said it in a nice way but sometimes he said it in a mean way. The bottom line is that we learned how to talk about what we were going through and be more real and intimate with each other and with pain. I learned to tell Kevin about my dreams and aspirations; even when in the past he had ignored, mocked, or seemed to not care about what I was saying. I stepped out in faith believing that God could change him and I just needed to be obedient even when Kevin didn't respond emotionally the way I always wanted.

The secrets and special moments we share in an affair are not really secrets; they are just layers of us that get buried in marriage due to busyness, defensiveness, hurt, unhealthy patterns of communication, and time constraints. In an affair the other person will always respond in more meaningful, respectful ways. They do not have the history with us that we share with our spouse, and in actuality we had those special moments when we were dating our spouse and were pursuing one another. In an affair the other person may have a different life experience or skill set that makes them more attentive in different areas, but the real issue is our choice to be vulnerable and real with them in intimate and deep ways. Anytime you are hiding away with another person one–on–one it is much easier to relax,

> *The counsel of another person in these situations cannot be overstated*

open up, and let your "real" self be known. It is the person dealing with the bills, the kids, the weight gain, the family dynamics, the errands, the laundry, and life that are hidden from us under the veil of routine and ritual. They are shrouded in layers of responsibility and it seems as if they have changed so much we don't even recognize them anymore. Perhaps they have, but the reality is that we as a couple have changed in the quality of our interactions, the quantity of our interactions, and the depth of our intimacy.

If we can train ourselves to be vulnerable again to our spouse in more meaningful, purposeful ways that matter to them, we may also be able to train them to learn to think deeper and react more maturely to us. When we withhold our true selves from our spouse we are denying them the opportunity to also grow and mature the way that God intended them to.

This is not an exhaustive list of strategies when dealing with adultery but it is a start. Lastly and perhaps the most important strategy when dealing with adultery is to seek help from outside sources. The counsel of another person in these situations cannot be overstated. Gaining perspective is critical to making the right decision about where you go in your relationship. It is also helpful to talk through bad days and make goals and dig deeper into the roadblocks you may face as you reconcile. It is not a quick fix and if you are approaching it that way you are setting yourself up for failure. Maybe not another affair but by missing the authentic connection and healing that could take place in your relationship and in you. Counseling is not a quick fix and there are many approaches available: crisis intensive counseling, ongoing weekly, or on an as needed basis. The key is a commitment to accountability of some sort to break the relationship through to a new level of hope and perspective.

It is also critical to find a support system through counseling or mentoring that supports your reconciliation and promotes marriage even when it is extremely difficult. This may be the time when those trusted friends you talked to so much in the past about what a jerk he is, or what a nag she is; will not be the ones you talk to about your reconciliation. They have tainted information that may cause a bias towards either you or your spouse. You need affirmative, Godly counsel and support–not the projection of other well meaning friends' anger and insecurity with their own life or your choice to recommit to marriage.

Adultery is the most obvious of hope busters but it does not have to destroy you or deplete your hope level. Take the time to try some of the strategies listed above to deal with the negative affects of adultery.

Taking it Home

1. How have you contributed to hope busting in your marriage? Be specific with attitude and action that you have done that has robbed your marriage of hope. (You may have done a combination of behaviors related to a variety of hope busters so name as many as you think you have done.)

2. Identify what has been the hope buster for you in your marriage (what action of your spouse has robbed you of hope or depleted hope?). In what way has that occurred? Now take a moment and compare it with what your spouse has identified.

3. Out of all these hope busters listed in the chapter above, what is the one that you need to change or seek help out of? Make a plan below on what strategy you will use to start fighting against this hope buster. Who will you use to help you with this? Be specific.

HOPE CHALLENGE

Out of all the hope busters that we have listed pick one that you know your spouse struggles with towards you. This week find a way to write a note and do a behavior that encourages your spouse that you are working on this issue and you do not expect them to fix this for you. (Make sure you are working on this issue and it is a tangible solution to the problem especially if it is a bigger problem.)

Chapter 4 – HOPE: A Formula For a Successful Marriage

Humility, Openness, Perseverance, Empathy

"The Lord is my portion says my soul, therefore I hope in HIM." Lamentations 3:24 NKJV

We now have a better understanding of what hope is, we know what can kill hope, so let's focus on the different dimensions of hope in marriage by breaking it down with a simple acronym, H.O.P.E. We know of course that a formulaic approach to marriage is not the answer but if we can keep it simple and easy to remember then we can access the approach more quickly. So let's begin by defining each of the words associated with this acronym.

H is for humility,

O is for openness,

P is for perseverance, and

E is for empathy.

HUMILITY

Are you a person of humility? To answer this correctly, we must truly understand what humility is. First let's break it down by examining the definition of humility. The Biblical definition of humility as used in both the Hebrew and the Greek ranges from meekness, lowliness and humbleness of mind, modesty, gentleness, to choose or prefer, and to delight in. The online Encarta dictionary defines it as "the quality of being modest or respectful." All of the meaning surrounding humility have to do with being considerate, preferring others above yourself, being polite, almost reverential. Now in the context of marriage, this feels like an almost impossible task. The reason it is so difficult is because we know what our spouse has done to us, how they have hurt us. At times it pains us to continue to approach them in a spirit of humility, it feels like an affront to the pain they have put upon us, and yet, dear friend, humility is a gateway attitude towards change. Why is this? To gain a better understanding, let's examine the antonym of humility: pride. Understanding pride is at the root of becoming a person of humility.

Pride is, "arrogance" or "appearing above others." When we are above another person, we are better simply because we believe we are better. Pride is not always obvious. It is driven from a heart that believes only in our way of doing things. It is proven with impatience and foolish talk. Proverbs 14:3 tells us *"In the mouth of a fool is a rod of pride, but the lips of the wise will preserve them."* NKJV

The mouth will always demonstrate if you have pride. In our marriage a way we can examine this is to ask ourselves the following questions?

- Do I make sure my spouse understands my position fully on everything when we are in conflict?

- Do I think my spouse's way of dealing with problems or conflicts is ridiculous at times and I don't take time to listen to it?

- Do I believe there is only one good way to deal with issues and it is usually my way?

- Do I get easily irritated and impatient with my spouse's ideas, suggestions, or hurts?

- Do I tend to "over talk" my spouse to make sure they hear my point?

If you answered yes to any of these then slow down and examine your heart for pride. Pride only works to divide. Even if your points are vastly superior to those of your spouse or your ideas make much more sense, sometimes sacrificing your comments or suggestions to your spouse can preserve and protect you from the pain that can rob hope. You see after it is all said and done, it is not a win to make your point because then you are only left with the awkward silence between you and your spouse when they are left believing they can never measure up to your wisdom or your goodness. Better to approach your spouse in the spirit of humility, preferring them above yourself, than to elevate yourself to a place where they cannot possibly reach you.

So how is humility tied into hope? Hope is the anticipation or expectation of something, remember? If you make your point by being prideful or pushy all the time with your spouse, your hope is not really in Christ. It is in your own ability to argue or communicate. This isn't saying do not communicate, do not let your spouse know how you are feeling; it is a heart examination. Look at your intent. Are you blasting back out of hurt? Are you feeling not listened to and need to make

> Humility is that opening for God to do the work, it is not lying down like a dog and doing nothing

him listen? Humility is that opening for God to do the work, it is not lying down like a dog and doing nothing, it is to trust in the sovereignty of God to work as HE sees fit in a conflict or crisis with your spouse; including if the work must be done in you. If you are trying to force a reaction out of your spouse then you are in charge of the outcome, not God.

Let's examine Romans 8:24 *"For in this hope we were saved. But hope that is seen is no hope at all. Who hopes for what he already has?"* NIV

If we actually believe in our own ability to effect change and we have in our minds the best–case scenario of what should happen, then we believe only in what we see or know to be true, and friend, we will be disappointed. What we see and expect are based on our own frame of reference and our own arguing ability, it is not based on the concept of surrender. However, true humility can let go of the outcome and can hope, or confidently expect, that God Himself has an interest and a stake in the outcome. Humility also allows God to do a work and bring about change in you, not just your spouse.

Humility as a tool for change within our marriage has been critical. We are both stubborn, passionate people, and it seems we were born for arguing. In the first eight years of our marriage neither one of us could back down during conflict, at least not until one person was mortally wounded. This was something we had to change when we got remarried and it is still a very important principle in our interactions. How we implemented it is by following a principle that seems to really release us from the grip of our anger. It is the principle we call "Do the opposite."

Do the Opposite

Simply put, if you believe it is within your nature to argue back, to raise your voice, to snap, or to shut down during conflict then you must do the opposite of your anticipated reaction. Not only is this a training tool to break bad habits, it is a spiritual discipline as well. The flesh or the physical realm always fails. Psalms 73:26 *"My flesh and my heart fail: but God is the strength of my heart and my portion forever."* NKJV

The hardest thing that we have had to break is our habits. These are not just physical habits like our body language, or verbal responses. These are also the thought patterns that we habitually choose to think during pain, crisis, or conflict with our spouse. So many times Kevin would take my frustration and pain as sending the message that he is a failure as a husband. His thought patterns were perpetually fed by habits of thinking, "I'll never measure up," or "I can't make her happy." When Kevin started to train his mind to think the opposite he would sometimes say out loud, "My wife just needs me to listen," and "Chris is not blaming me for this. She is just venting pain." This thought pattern change, coupled with an opposite behavioral choice, creates an environment of humility and change.

I was able to minister to Kevin by literally being quiet. There were so many times in our marriage that I would use destructive words like, "Why can't you just understand me?" or "I see why people get a divorce." In my mind these were just statements of truth, but they were words that were feeding Kevin's sense of being a failure. I used to say, "Well, don't you want me to tell you how I feel?" But there was no buffer or filter that my feelings went through. I didn't fully understand Hebrews 4:12 which tells us *For the Word of God is living and powerful and sharper than any two edged sword, piercing even to the division of soul and spirit, and of joints and marrow, and is a discerner of the thoughts and intents of the heart."* NKJV

I didn't appreciate that the word of God could really help me see into my deepest thoughts, and my deepest thoughts were that I was trying to motivate Kevin by shaming him. If only he could see that I was miserable then maybe he would change.

Of course it is important that your spouse know how you feel but before you tell them it is more important that you know what is at the root of those feelings. What is the core hurt or the driving motivation for telling all to your spouse? Often times for me it was so he could make me feel better or so I could get him to change his mind. I had a faulty and broken perspective on marriage that if I felt better, and we got along all the time then my marriage was good. Marriage cannot create an environment where two people "feel good" all the time. It is impossible; but because of my painful experience of my parents' marriage, I truly wanted a marriage that was more fantasy than reality. I did not understand that feelings are not the guide to marital intimacy. They are indicators of pain and the need for change, but not true reflectors of my marriage stability. I had

> *Openness can build upon the foundation of hope*

to relearn ways to manage my feelings and emotions and then respectfully voice my needs to Kevin, or just remain quiet and pray that God would change him instead. Humility allowed both of us to learn to put the other one above us. In doing so, we were open for hope to do its work; we were softened in our hearts to confidently expect God's goodness to be demonstrated through our spouse. And in the end we were humbled that God could use us to deeply impact the life of our spouse.

Openness

Openness can build upon the foundation of hope. By creating an honest and authentic truth base in a marriage, we can confidently expect God to work in meaningful ways in our union. Openness implies that there is earnest, serious, and genuine attempts at communication. How often in marriage do we shut down? This is a serious matter for us to consider as we communicate with our spouse. Because each of us are used to certain interactions with our spouse, we tend to communicate in a certain manner about certain things. By doing this we are not being open, we are hiding behind the mask of habitual and comfortable communication, more than likely because we are afraid or unsure of our spouse's reaction to us, or because we know the predicted response they will give us.

We often mistake harsh and blunt communication with open and candid communication. They are not the same. The purpose of openness is to release truth, to speak candidly and deliberately with your mate in order to promote the expectation that they will receive from you. In doing so the change will come in either one of you as God sees necessary. In harsh and blunt communication the end result is making the point of being heard for the sake of being heard. In Paul's letter to the Ephesians in chapter four he is addressing the issue of unity within the body of Christ, he starts out with the admonition for humbleness, but as he gets further into his letter in verse 15 he says *"Instead, speaking the truth in love, we will in all things grow up into Him who is the head, that is Christ."* NLT

We are directed in the body of Christ to strive towards unity and growing up, and in doing this one of our tools is to speak the truth.

Speak the Truth

"You're so emotional." "You're a slob. Can't you keep anything organized?" "You're always late." "Your family is so dysfunctional." "You never listen." All these statements may feel like truth to you but when evaluated on their merit alone, they are actually judgments. The truth is about the veracity of a situation–the reality and actuality of life. Truth, as we learned in Ephesians 4, as used in a biblical sense, is to promote unity within a relationship and grow us closer to Jesus Christ. Is what you're saying to your spouse going to promote a oneness between the two of you and bring you closer to Christ?

To answer this question we must first ask ourselves, do we really know our spouse? What is their frame of reference, their family of origin experience, and the reasons they may act the way they do? Deeper yet, do we see with an eye of the spirit, understanding what ingrained patterns and habits our spouse is struggling with, rather then judging their actions, attitudes, and responses as a personal accusation or an offense against us? Perhaps an overly emotional spouse is actually a person who lived in a home where emotions were predominant and the only way they were heard is through emotional expressiveness, or they weren't heard if they were emotionally expressive. Or perhaps you lived in a house where neatness was not important so therefore you never learned to organize. Many patterns are actually just learned behaviors, habits, or ways of doing things that are not deliberately against another person. In evaluating how, and when, you speak the truth or use openness in your relationship with your spouse take the time to make a list of all the situations or times when you are not open and ask yourself your motivation behind it.

Openness is tied into motivation. Many arguments that are wide open and destructive, where we let it all hang out, are primarily motivated by selfishness. With Kevin and I it was about making a point to the other person, somehow forcing their hand to get them to listen to see it our way. It failed every time. Why? Because as we look at openness in the Bible we see that when Jesus or any of His followers used "truth" it was always with the intent to restore the person. The motivation when Jesus spoke to the woman at the well about her sin was not to shame her and show His ultimate superiority, rather it was to help her see the pain that her life was causing. Her relationships with men were interfering with her relationship with God and ultimately in her witness to others. Jesus was merely an instrument used to restore her relationship with the Father God.

So when we talk about openness with our spouse, again the challenge is to be motivated by the truth bringing freedom. If the secrets you have been hiding from your spouse are causing a lack of unity and possibly a lack of accountability for you then it is important to be open with them. In doing so you may be bringing them to a deeper walk with God because they are confronted with pain that can only be healed through Jesus and His transforming work within them. It is important to evaluate if a third party should be present to help facilitate or coach a discussion where you need to reveal something to your spouse. Often times we need the guidance of another fellow supporter who can help us tell our secrets tactfully and help our spouse receive the truth with grace.

Kevin kept his drinking from me for a number of years, he wasn't open because he knew it was a destructive choice and I would not approve. He also knew I would judge him harshly and not be supportive. After our reconciliation we spoke of this with a trusted minister and within the confines of how we would build accountability and boundaries in our relationship for the future. The conversation was

> Often times we need the guidance of another fellow supporter

not about me condemning him for his choices but rather for us to be brought into unity about the reality of how bad our marriage had gotten. We both had a role in the breakdown of our communication and although he was the one that chose to drink, I had created an environment of hostility where honesty was greeted with judgment, not love. Openness brings hope because it facilitates trust between the two of you again. If our spouse is a person we can trust to be real with us then the hope comes because the expectation of honesty is met.

Perseverance

Often times with hope, we are not talking about an empty promise of something good happening someday. It is an active anticipation or expectation as stated in chapter one. This doesn't imply that the thing, which we anticipate, will occur in our time frame. We are told in Isaiah 55 that God's ways are above our ways and His thoughts above our thoughts. (See Isaiah 55:8–9). We all know His timing is also out of our complete realm of understanding, and yet, we can believe that He has our best interest in mind. We do this through perseverance of hope. This principle if applied in marriage can also help us shed our expectation of the timing in which we expect things to happen.

Perseverance, according to the New Oxford American Dictionary is both a noun and a verb. This does tell us that it is both a thing and an action we must engage in. The definition is "steadfastness in doing something despite difficulty or delay in achieving success" (noun) and "to continue in a course of action even in the face of difficulty" (verb). What this demonstrates to us is that there must be a shift in our mind, first, to accept this thing we call perseverance and then second, a corresponding shift in our actions to choose the path in continuing something difficult. Sometimes that difficult thing is our marriage. When we face a challenge in our marriage that threatens to rob us of our hope, we have the choice to be steadfast in our commitment to persevere and then we also have the choice to choose the course of action that will feed the persevering attitude.

The Link Between Perseverance and Obedience

Paul tells us in Philippians 3:14 *"I press towards the mark for the prize of the high calling of God in Christ Jesus."* NKJV

Paul had hope that no matter what his circumstances God was doing something valuable in his life, through him, and for others. We too must adopt this attitude in marriage. Through our perseverance, not just in attitude but also in action, we can fuel hope that our marriage can be successful. Paul did eventually die a martyr's death. The thing is he never saw his life as less than valuable nor did he fail. He wrote the epistles and groomed so many others of Jesus' followers; much of this was done through perseverance. He chose an attitude when he was converted and from there he changed the corresponding action to be one of obedience to Jesus Christ and His message.

This may sound super spiritual and like we are all called to die. There is much truth in the statement that we are called to die in marriage, but really what we are trying to demonstrate is that through perseverance in attitude, with corresponding action,

> *As you obey and persevere, you become fueled by hope, which then leads to further obedience*

you will receive hope. The hope will not be a false feeling. It will be fed by the act of obedience, the knowledge that pressing toward a mark, or goal, you have in your relationship with Christ and in your marriage, will be achieved by doing what God has told you to do. That is such a hopeful statement.

As you obey and persevere, you become fueled by hope, which then leads to further obedience. Your aim is no longer to get what you can out of marriage or to just hang in there for the kids. Your aim is to persevere for something greater. That something greater is obedience to God's calling on your life; not so you can play the martyr for sticking it out in a hopeless marriage but so that you can achieve the greater prize in Christ Jesus. We doubt Paul just kept looking back in regret and hopelessness about his life, but rather he pressed on through every trial and became even more gifted and reached more people because of it.

Identify the Persevering Action

The key between perseverance and hope is to find the corresponding persevering action that enables you to obey God. For us it was making a commitment to change some very destructive ways of talking to one another. I might talk about divorce or even be tempted to reflect on my glory days when Kevin and I weren't together. Kevin may be tempted to see me as the ice princess or cold wife that he used to. When we adopt a persevering attitude we then change our behavior and our communication. We don't say those things no matter how tempting it is. Instead of sneaking off in silence and sulking for days by myself, I choose to stick around and not run away. It is much easier for me to hide, go for a long overnight or multiple night drive and shut down, than it is to talk or stay put and use eye contact. My persevering action is to stay put, force eye contact and physical touch, and resolve the discussion as much as we can. We each have actions that are out of our normative reaction that we can choose to implement and make persevering actions. The choice is ours to really evaluate what those actions are for us, and then commit to do them as much as possible.

As Romans 5:4 tells us *"and endurance develops strength of character in us, and character strengthens our confident expectation of salvation."* NLT

Perseverance will start to seem less like work as you see the rewards you feel when you stick with a course of action and act like the person you know you want to be in marriage. When you obey in marriage you know God approves and the end result is more hope.

Empathy

Empathy has been very misunderstood in relationships because it is often associated with an ambiguous feeling that is hard to articulate. Simply put it is the ability to understand and share the feelings of another (Oxford American Dictionary). We often feel like we cannot understand our spouse's feelings because they are so different from us. Empathy allows us the freedom to try. Other words for empathy are compassion and sympathy. Break these down even further and you see that kindness, consideration, concern, and care are all part of the big picture of empathy. It sounds a lot like the components we want to find in love but if we break it down to a simple level, it makes it easier for us to put empathy into action.

Empathy Must Result in Action

What does care look like? Is it a special understanding of your spouse's love language and meeting that need? Is it just touching their face because they like to have their hair stroked? Is it having dinner made because you know your spouse enjoys a hot meal? Care is borne out of love and love has many facets. I Corinthians 13 lays out for us the picture of that perfect agape love we all want to have. However, we fall short at times in understanding the bigger dimensions of love like how it is longsuffering, patient, kind, not rejoicing in wrong. It is important for us to actually define ways that we empathize with our spouse. As we do this it will also feed our hope.

Proverbs 13:12 tells us *"hope deferred makes the heart sick but when the desire comes it is a tree of life."* NKJV

In a relationship we all long to be understood and to be loved. That is why we get married. Our hope is that our spouse will love us unconditionally and not do those things that contribute to hope busting. When we hope, for what seems like forever, for a change in our spouse, we can get sick in our souls. We feel unfulfilled; we have missed that tree of life so to speak. But by utilizing empathy–a genuine understanding of the feelings of another, we can look deeper at the hurts and rifts in the heart of our spouse. The empathy allows us to share in their pain, to properly understand it and to then put our love into action. Depending on our spouse's experience, maybe we love them more by holding them, by writing letters, being more confrontive with them instead of holding back, doing a physical activity with them, initiating sexual relationship more, praying for them, or attending church with them. Again the effort is made to utilize empathy for where your spouse is at in order to promote the hope level. It doesn't always work to change the spouse, but the end result arethe changes within you.

Love Covers Sin

The motivator for your spouse then is not your nagging but your love and empathy. I Peter 4:8 tells us *"Above all things have fervent love for one another for love will cover a multitude of sins."* NKJV

We are not told that love just dismisses the sins, it tells us that it covers the sin. The Greek word for cover is "kalupto", and it literally means to hide (Strong's Exhaustive Concordance). This means that we keep the sin out of sight of others or out of their view or notice. How often do we want people to notice how hard it is with our spouse, or how bad they have hurt us, especially when it has been an obvious hurt like adultery or financial failure or something that is very painful to deal with year after year. This verse does not tell us to hide these things from the world if we need help for them, or to hide them in order to protect the spouse. It is literally telling us that we must first examine our love level; do we have fervent love first and foremost towards one another? If we cannot evaluate ourselves and say that we have loved our spouse in ways that the Bible instructs then we must look first at ourselves and what actions we can take to love deeper and understand greater.

So again break down empathy into action steps to show care, compassion, and understanding. Are there times your spouse has said "you never" or "you always" right before they told you something that really bothered them about you? If so then that is a good starting point. Is there an action point you could take to show your spouse that you are moving forward and changing in your love and empathy towards them? Usually your best clues are found in what motivates your spouse. However, remember that the primary goal behind empathy and love is not to get what you want, it is to minister to your spouse in a totally different way by emptying yourself and not drawing attention to their faults and sins in the marriage.

Fill Yourself With Love

If you are filled with love you will be able to minister to your spouse with the love it calls for in 1 Corinthians 13 and I Peter 4. It will be important for you to find ways that you connect with God and His love whether it is through nature, exercise, a hobby, creative outlets, volunteering, writing, or going out with a friend and talking. If you connect with God's love for

> If you connect with God's love for you it allows you to pour love into your spouse freely with no expectation of return

you it allows you to pour love into your spouse freely with no expectation of return. Our hope is that there is a return. The dynamic of love poured out is that hope is fueled in the marriage and both are loving one another. This is the power of empathy when properly understood. It is perhaps the strongest force to motivate a spouse. It was, after all, what Christ did for us to bring us the promise of relationship with Him. Therefore it makes sense that it should also be a powerful force in bringing hope to the most hopeless of marriages and the most dismal of situations.

One of the ways that we used empathy to bring hope into our situation when we were reconciling was through the power of the written letter to one another. Kevin wrote me letters during our divorce but they weren't just nice letters to make me feel good, they were letters of understanding. Instead of accusing me of all the hurtful things I had said and done in our previous marriage he chose to tell me how he wished he had tried harder to understand the hurt I experienced as a child. He reached into a very uncomfortable territory by trying to see how my past childhood experiences had deeply wounded me in ways that I couldn't always articulate in the marriage. I had reasons for running away from our fights; I had reasons also for shutting down completely and pushing him away through condemnation. Now understand this, they were reasons and not excuses. I used them as excuses because I did not try to get help or change them. I instead shifted blame onto Kevin for hurting me by not understanding me. Empathy allowed Kevin to try to tell me what he witnessed as my frailties and hurts and allowed him to look beyond my reactions in our marriage to the missing parts of me. He then could identify ways that he could actually love me that would be meaningful for my experiences. He wrote because that was something tangible I could hold onto; I had never had that. He did acts of service for me because I never experienced a father taking care of me. Through understanding brought action motivated from love. The end result was my hope level changed. I grew from harboring bitterness towards him to actually expecting or believing that we could remarry again. This is a cycle that we continue to this day in order to bring hope to the marriage through empathy.

Humility, openness, perseverance, and empathy are four keys that we have identified that can feed hope and change your marriage. Throughout the Bible we see these four traits identified in Jesus and His followers so it is critical for us to emulate them in our marriage relationship as well.

Taking it Home

1. Out of the four traits identified in the above chapter what is the one you demonstrate the best in your marriage? How do you demonstrate it? What can you do to improve on it?

2. Out of the four traits identified in the above chapter which one do you need to work on practicing more? Specifically what do you need to do in order to practice that trait?

3. Which one of these traits would minister or mean the most to your spouse? How would it minister to them (behavior, action or attitude)?

4. Which one of these traits would mean the most or minister to you? How would it minister to you (behavior, action or attitude)?

HOPE CHALLENGE

Each of these four traits had actions that complimented them, pick an action from one of them that you will do this week to minister to your spouse. (i.e apologize more or first, be the first to share instead of shutting down, use an empathetic statement to show you truly understand instead of blowing them off) Write down your action and do it as much as possible without telling your spouse what it is.

Chapter 5 – Hope & Spiritual Leadership

"Wives, submit to your husbands as to the Lord. For the husband is the head of the wife as Christ is the head of the church, His body, of which He is the Savior. Now as the church submits to Christ, so also wives should submit to their husbands in everything. Husbands, love your wives, just as Christ loved the church and gave himself up for her to make her holy, cleansing her by the washing with water through the word, and to present her to Himself as a radiant church, without stain or wrinkle or any other blemish, but holy and blameless." Ephesians 5:22–27 NIV

This chapter is going to be one of the most important for hope building in the marriage and family. A lot of the focus in this chapter will be on the husband, but the wife has her own particular role in supporting her husband's spiritual leadership that is vastly different than his role. I am so excited about all that God has for men in the realm of spiritual leadership. Generally, when we think of the spiritual leader, we must specifically look to the husband in the marriage relationship.

Sadly, so many Christian men do not have the understanding or training to be the leader in the home. I'm not talking about the specific understanding of being a leader as the financial provider; I'm talking about understanding the fundamental needs, tools, and responsibilities of the spiritual leader for the family.

Isn't Leadership an Instinct?

Men are born with the instinct to be the provider and protector of the family, but we need the training in order

> *Men are born with the instinct to be the provider and protector of the family*

to be equipped to lead in the capacity that God intends us to lead. His plan for Adam was to be leading alongside Eve in the marriage, but with the authority as the head of the house. This headship has been greatly misunderstood within the walls of the church over the past 2000 years, and the disparity in the descriptions range from:

1.   The head of the house who rules over the family, like a dictator and with an "IRON FIST" so to speak.

2.   The head of the house is no longer needed today, men are like women, and if man tries to rule he will then dominate the wife and there will be no equality.

Neither of these two descriptions above are what God intended for the leader of his family. God intended there to be a husband and a wife, both equal in value, but with very different job descriptions and responsibilities. We see in Ephesians 5 that the husband is called to lead as the head of his wife, as Christ is head over the church. This is not a dictatorship role, and it is very misunderstood in the body of Christ. *It is clear to me that Paul is speaking of husbands that are becoming Christ like and continually pursuing to live like Christ did.* The parallel between Christ's relationship with the church and the husband's relationship with the wife is clear. This is the formula for the model marriage, where the wife submits (or comes underneath the leadership) to the husband that is actively and continually living a Christian life to the best of his ability.

Let's take a moment to breakdown the word submission by looking at Strong's Exhaustive Concordance:

Submit

hupotassō—greek word

hoop–ot–as'–so

to*subordinate*; reflexively to *obey:* – be under obedience (obedient), put under, subdue unto, (be, make) subject (to, unto), be (put) in subjection

---

The Greek word for submission here, "hupotasso," is also used as a military word for coming under in obedience. Paul used this Greek word in verse 22 for a reason, and it was to describe what this submission by a wife to her husband looks like. If you think about how a general leads men and women that fall below him in rank, under his leadership, you can better understand this word submit in verse 22. The men and women that are under a general's leadership have a respect for that leadership and understand that he is not a dictator but a wise and gifted leader. For the most part, these people are following orders from him because they do respect the authority of the office even if they don't always understand all of his decisions.

Leadership is Sacrifice

Even as Christians, we forget this part of Paul's command to marriages. So often, Christians see these verses as a call for women to be weak and dominated by men. Christ sacrificed for the body and laid his life down for us so that we could have eternal life. We as husbands are called to sacrifice for our wives, and that is not a characteristic of a dictator. The character of a dictator is to overpower, punish, and demean another. Again, Paul is not describing women as lower than men, just that they are different in many respects. For example, our bodies are very different, from appearance to strength, and our emotional capacity for nurturing and problem solving are also widely varied. Women are generally better equipped for caregiving and can adapt to nurturing situations often more easily than men. Whereas men tend to fix or want to bring a solution to the "problem" at hand rather than immediately jump to an emotional response. Men are generally more adept at problem solving issues that can be easily remedied through calculations. Whereas women have the capability to evaluate the underlying meaning of what seem like logical problems. These differences highlight our uniqueness and amplify our ability to fulfill our God given roles. So from this point on, no matter what you have heard about the submission of wives to their husbands, I'm asking that you look very objectively at what I am saying about these verses. Please don't take my word for it, do some studying and your own research and with the help of the Holy Spirit, make your own evaluation of these roles between a husband and a wife.

Be in the Word

In verse 26, the husband is called to do as Christ does with the church, sanctifying her and cleansing her, and washing her with the water of the word. I believe men, this is a command for us to be in the word and knowing the word so that we are able to lead our wife and family the way that Christ leads us. But men, I cannot expect Chris to come under my leadership if I do not first apply myself as that leader. This does mean being in the word, understanding the word, understanding my responsibility to God as the leader, and being in prayer so that I can hear from the Lord on how to do my job as a spiritual leader.

This is not an option guys, it is a command as a husband

This is not an option guys, it is a command as a husband. I can't tell you how many men I have talked to that just want the fringe benefits of being the leader and a husband. It saddens me exponentially that so many men in the church are trying to lead by force, rather than by example. Christ leads us by example and so that is where we have to look to lead our family. There is nowhere in the Bible that says that we can have the option as to whether the husband is the spiritual leader or if the wife should take this role. However, Chris and I see more often than not, that the wife is forced to try to lead her family spiritually because the husband is handing the role over to her. Commonly, she is the one who initiates going to church or any church related events. She is often the one teaching her children the ways of the Bible and what Christianity is all about.

Don't get me wrong. She has an equal role in teaching the children about Jesus and modeling a Christian wife. But so many times we see the man just kind of checking out when it comes to the spiritual leadership role in the marriage. This often leads to hopelessness in the marriage and it definitely affects the example that the children need in their father. The boys then often learn to be passive when it comes to the Christian walk, allowing mom, and eventually their wife to lead in the home spiritually. The girls then learn to take the reins when it comes to spiritual leadership in their marriage and also seek out men that don't walk in the understanding of their role as a husband/spiritual leader. This is exactly where I had taken my family on our first marriage and the results were evident in my wife and in my son. They resented me and did not have true respect for me since I was not acting in a way worthy of respect.

It is so easy for hopelessness to creep into the marriage when the roles are not healthy between the husband and the wife. The picture does not get more hopeful, the more the wife is trying to lead, because it is not the way God intended it, and therefore it just becomes more of a burden for her to carry. This can eventually lead to bitterness and hurt from the wife towards the husband. There is such a balance to be struck in understanding the strength that each spouse brings to the marriage and not taking advantage of the wife's strength if it appears she is better at leading. The essential question to evaluate within yourself men is do you view spiritual leadership as power or being a servant?

Friend, if you have been under the impression that a husband has power over his wife, respectfully, you are misled and this could actually be considered abuse. God has an awesome plan for the husband and wife to lead the family together, but with each following their respective roles according to the Bible. The men are clearly called to serve and to sacrifice by example. This doesn't imply that they are "whipped" by their wives or that their wife "wears the pants" in the family. This tells us that men are called to be Godly, they are humble, and they lead through Godly example.

Changing This Dynamic

First and foremost, we have to lead by this Biblical example as clarified above. Paul's writings in Ephesians 5:22–27 and Colossians 3:18 are just some basics to lead by. In Genesis 3:16 it says *"Unto the woman He said, I will greatly multiply thy pain and thy conception; in pain thou shalt bring forth children; and thy desire shall be to thy husband, and he shall rule over thee."* ASV

What we seem to run into here is an issue of translation, or language. Men and women see the word RULE and right off the bat there is misunderstanding by a lot of Christians. The husband says, "See honey, it says right here that I will rule over you," and she sees the word RULE and is intimidated or just plain angry at the role God has given her in the marriage.

Here is how I interpret it; she will naturally desire him as he leads the way Christ leads us, and she will naturally desire to be under his authority as she sees him operate as God established him to operate. It gets a little tricky here. Chris and I are constantly

> *She will naturally desire him as he leads the way Christ leads us*

asked the question, "What if he is not leading as the Bible commands?" or "Can't I start submitting after I see him lead the way Christ does?" Our answer follows 1 Peter 3:1 *"In like manner, ye wives, be in subjection to your own husbands; that, even if any obey not the word, they may without the word be gained by the behavior of their wives."* ASV

This call to wives is to be an example to the husband of what a Godly wife looks like. This does not mean that she has to be subject to abuse. Wives, you can impact him by the way that you live under him, and the Holy Spirit can move through your example without you having to teach him with words. This does not mean that you can't communicate about the real issues, or that you have to just sit by and watch things happen that are not healthy. I believe that the author is saying that wives can show the love and example of Christ by living it out day to day. Sometimes it requires words and sometimes it does not. Using Godly discretion will help guide your decisions in how this impact is made.

Husbands, it is very important that you do not take responsibility for her spiritual walk. Yes, you need to be the example and direct your family so that they have the opportunity to grow in Christ, but you can't live it for her. Have grace for where she is at and again, lead by example. She wants to follow a respected leader, not a controlling dictator.

How Do We Do This?

Spiritual leadership must be applied consistently in order to build hope and give direction for the marriage the way we are called to do it in the Bible. Jesus said,

> *Matthew 6:33 But seek ye first his kingdom, and his righteousness; and all these things shall be added unto you. ASV*

Jesus is giving us the ultimate tool here, that we would seek Him so that we can live our daily lives with His help. This applies to being in, and understanding the word too. We need to be looking to the Bible, the tool God gave us to understand Him better, so that we can operate with the wisdom that He gives freely. As we are in the Word, the sins and unhealthy thought patterns in our own life will become more evident to us, allowing us to see the need for repentance and change to take place so that we can continually grow in our Christian walk. It is much easier to receive conviction from the Holy Spirit as you are consistently seeking His wisdom, than it is to receive what may seem like nagging from your wife.

David gives us a great example in the Psalms of putting our hope in God continually in Psalms 71:14 *"but I will hope continually, and will praise thee yet more and more."* ASV

Look at the word YET in that verse, David is telling us that even when things feel hopeless, he is going to continue to praise more and more, if for no other reason than just to build his hope. He is practicing his spiritual walk, and is using his praise now to demonstrate it.

Stay Connected to Other Believers

John 15:4, *"Remain united to me, and I will remain united to you. A branch cannot bear fruit by itself; it can do so only if it remains in the vine. In the same way you cannot bear fruit unless you remain in me."* ASV

We need to get our family involved in church. This looks different for every family depending on circumstances, but it is a must. We need the leadership and authority of a pastor as one source for receiving Biblical teaching. Find a church home where you feel the Holy Spirit is moving and where you can be taught the

Word of God. So many families get too busy for church and this is such a sad scenario. They feel that they can just read the Word and learn on their own, but the body of Christ, or a church family, is important for accountability, training, and fellowship. If you feel like you can have your own church at home take a moment to examine your life and your pride. Jesus always found growth in His alone time with the Father and with community with others. If His greatest commandment is to love others, the best way to practice that love is in the community of other believers.

Lastly, and what I have found to be critical in my own ability to spiritually lead my family is accountability with other men. This must be authentic accountability where honest experiences and struggles can be shared and wisdom can be sought. None of us can do this on our own. We need the wisdom of those that have gone before us to help us to develop a healthy understanding of the Word. I do this by praying once a week with a prayer partner and being transparent about my walk with Jesus and the struggles I go through in my marriage and my walk.

Spiritual leadership is a gift you can give your spouse. Men, you are called to be like Christ. He is the ultimate giver. Ask yourself today to have Him transform you. You can bring hope to your marriage through your example, your walk with God, and your leadership.

Taking it Home

1. What would you define spiritual leadership as? Be as specific as you can here.

2. Do you see any patterns in your marriage where the wife is having to try to fill the spiritual leadership role? If so, identify what is happening. What do you need to do to take this responsibility back? Be specific.

3. Be honest guys, can you relate in any way to feeling that the husband should have power over his wife? If so, in what areas do you feel you have portrayed this? Wives, in what way have you experienced this power?

4. In what ways do you need to step up as the spiritual leader? Are you in the word? Are you in prayer? What needs to change in order to better live in this role that God has given you?

(What is your action plan for change?) Wives, how can you support your husband in this effort?

HOPE CHALLENGE

This week as you are reflecting on the roles you each have in the marriage, think about how you can bring hope back into the relationship through fulfilling your Biblical role. (ex. Men, initiate going to church this week if this is not something you usually do. Ladies, pray for him in an area of conflict where you would generally confront the issue more aggressively.)

Chapter 6 – Hope and Forgiveness

"For there is hope for a tree, if it is cut down; that it will sprout again" Job 14:7 NKJV

In Job's struggle to understand the calamity that had fallen on him he wrestled with God over the meaning of his immense trials. It seemed in Chapter 14 that Job had reached a point where he felt like a tree could be brought back to life, but he truly questioned if a man could. He was struggling with how to navigate his way through the pain that his trials caused him. This is how unforgiveness is for us. It is a weight, invisible at times, difficult to understand, and harder yet to articulate. It seems as if life goes on around us, trees blossom again, flowers bloom in the spring, people go on living; but we feel smothered by the heaviness of the pain and trapped by the knowledge of the offense done against us and our inability to deal with it.

It is an unmistakable fact that unforgiveness is directly tied to our hope level, especially in marriage. Hope is an expectation, desire or anticipation therefore if

140

what we expect is the same response, the same empty interaction with our spouse because we haven't let go of the pain they caused us, then that is what we will get. Hopelessness then is one of the natural byproducts of unforgiveness. Conversely, hope and change are the natural byproducts of forgiveness. This is demonstrated throughout Scripture.

Examine the Bible

Mark 2:7, Luke 7:47, and Colossians 2:13, are all examples of the power of forgiveness to bring hope, and ultimately change. First, let's examine the gospel of Mark, we see the story of the paralytic who Jesus forgives, but does not immediately heal. The scribes' reaction was that of shock. How dare He forgive this man his sins. Jesus makes the point that there is more power and meaning in forgiveness than there is being able to walk. He does eventually heal the paralytic man and sends him home walking, but the power of forgiveness is what truly changed the man's life and had the most impact on those around him.

> *Hope and change are the natural byproducts of forgiveness*

The same holds true with the story in Luke 7 where Jesus goes to eat with the Pharisees. While Jesus is eating dinner, an unknown woman washes His feet with her tears and her hair. The Pharisees, namely Simon, question her character and ask Jesus to be careful for He doesn't really know what this woman is about. Jesus blows them away by talking about forgiveness; He asks them about debt and if He forgave two debts of differing values–one very large and one quite small–then which debtor would love Him more. Of course the conclusion is that the bigger debt that was forgiven elicited a more loving response to the forgiver. Jesus was making the point that this woman of lowly reputation was aware of her own abundant sin (debt) and she sought forgiveness. When Jesus turned to her and forgave her He said *"Your faith has saved you go in peace." Luke 7:50* NKJV

Through the power of forgiveness, her entire life was transformed. What began as an interaction of tears became a life full of peace **and hope**.

Forgiveness Changes Us

And so there are many examples in the Bible where forgiveness transforms and brings hope. The underlying message is that forgiveness changes us; both if we are forgiving, and if we forgive. You may be saying, "Well yeah, but that is Christ forgiving me. I just don't know if I can forgive my spouse for their _____ (fill in the blank)". The good news is that you don't have to pardon them alone, you need only to rely on Christ to do it for you. This sounds like a fix all approach and we don't say it lightly. We know that He is the forgiver of sins and since His spirit lives within us He gives us the ability to impart true forgiveness to our spouse when they have really torn us apart. We will talk more on that later once we truly understand what forgiveness is.

What Is Forgiveness?

According to the Webster's New College Dictionary the definitions of forgiveness are:

1. To excuse for a fault or offense: pardon

2. To renounce (to give up or reject) anger or resentment against

3. To absolve (clear of blame or guilt, relieve of a requirement or obligation) from payment of a debt. To accord forgiveness–to grant free pardon for or remission

In the New Testament the word forgive is used twenty–one times, and there are three distinct Greek words with varying definitions for it.

1. Aphiemi–cry, forgive, forsake, lay aside, leave, omit, put (send) away, remit, suffer, yield up

2. Apoluo –to free fully, relieve, release, dismiss or let die, depart, divorce, let go, set at liberty

3. Charizomai–to grant as a favor, in kindness pardon or rescue: deliver, give, grant

To truly grasp the power of forgiveness, we must internalize these meanings for ourselves, and learn to apply it to our situation. What we see as a common theme in each of these definitions is that forgiveness is a choice. How we walk that choice out is the difficult part.

Forgive and Forget?

Rooted in the definition of forgiveness is the inherent idea of making a conscious effort to put the memory out of your reach, or in other words to forget the impact the memory has on us. Forgetting a wrong done to you does not mean that you will never feel the sting of that pain or the humiliation of the act. Rather it can be looked at as leaving something behind intentionally, to banish from one's thoughts, failing to mention, or to neglect to become aware of something at the proper specified moment (See Webster's Dictionary). When understood in this light it is clear that the offense may never leave our conscious memory but that we can participate in how that offense becomes a part of our active thought life. It is also interesting that forgiveness may require multiple occasions of having to put a hurt or offense out of our mind when it comes up for us. This is such a freeing statement because it gives us the power to relinquish the angry and unforgiving thoughts, rather than dealing with the burden of feeling guilt if we have them.

We know that if we are dealing with a hope buster in our marriage that elicits pain and devastation within our spirit, then forgiving will not be easy. This chapter on forgiveness is not written to make it seem like a fix all or to make the problem seem less painful than it is, rather it is to help gain understanding on how forgiveness can actually promote hope, not just for you, but for the person you have forgiven. Forgiveness garners hope through the power of letting go. This act is only achieved through knowing Jesus Christ and His great act of pardon for us on the cross. It is not a guilt trip to say that we should forgive because Christ forgave us; it is a revelation when we feel the release to actually let go of what that person did to us. The revelation **is not** that the person we are forgiving is amazing, deserving and will change. The truth is that through the surrender of our unforgiveness we are moving closer to being like Christ.

Forgiveness Opens the Door to Prayers Being Answered

We are also allowing the mountains in our life to move. Mark 11:22–26 tells of the necessity of forgiveness. "So Jesus answered and said to them, have faith in God. For assuredly, I say to you whoever says to this mountain, Be removed and be cast into the sea, and does not doubt in his heart, but believes that those things he says will be done, he will have whatever he says. Therefore I say to you whatever things you ask when you pray, believe that you receive them and you will have them. And whenever you stand praying, if you have anything against anyone, forgive him that your Father in heaven may also forgive you your trespasses. But if you do not forgive, neither will your father in Heaven forgive your trespasses." NKJV

This revelation allows us to see that when we have unforgiveness it will be hard for us to pray and see results. So it is important to ask yourself about your prayer life and check for unforgiveness. During the process of rebuilding after infidelity, addictions, or just the pain of compounded wounds with our spouse, we have to evaluate our forgiveness capacity. There are times we feel weak, we don't see the possibility of forgiving our spouse or we perceive forgiveness as giving up. By gaining the proper understanding of what forgiveness is, and how we will walk it out, will give us a sense of freedom and purpose.

How to Walk Out Forgiveness

For instance, do we have to get back together with an adulterous spouse if they are sorry? Or do we take a spouse back who went to treatment and quit drinking or using drugs? Do we take a spouse back who has an anger and rage problem that has affected our life and the lives of our children? Do we choose to forgive a spouse who has habitually neglected us and ignored us and let us down in little ways that have compounded?

Well, once we understand that forgiveness is a restorative and freeing act that can only be granted by Jesus, but walked out by us, we can then decide to open our hearts to that change that God desires to bring in us to make that decision. The answer to those difficult questions can then reveal

Have I done everything I can to make this marriage work?

themselves to us as we live out our relationship with Christ. Until we know Jesus has touched our hearts and we have accepted His forgiveness, it will be hard to know how to impart that forgiveness to an "undeserving" spouse.

Keep in mind that the question we must always ask ourselves when considering how to walk in forgiveness is, "Have I done everything I can to make this marriage work?" If you can answer that with an emphatic yes then you may not be struggling with unforgiveness. This is between you and God. However, if you choose to accept that spouse back after adultery, or any other offense, and you say you are forgiving; this means that you are on a difficult road. The thoughts will come to draw you to the offense, and then your mind will have to make a deliberate effort to put it out of your thoughts. No, do not dismiss hurt, fear, and lack of trust but instead find ways to tell your spouse about your feelings and defeat the enemy. The pain compounds as you allow the thoughts to overwhelm you and you use your imagination to think about the situation. We all know when we are letting our thoughts go and reliving painful experiences; taking that extra step to confess the thoughts and seek prayer or even counsel at the time is necessary in learning to let go.

Again we are saying that true heart forgiveness may take multiple occasions of putting it out of your mind until the pain of that thought or memory no longer haunts you or overpowers you. Many people use tools like journals to express their thoughts or losses, some talk it over with a friend, others go to counseling, while some need to take medication such as antidepressants for a time to help them walk through the pain. The result you are looking for in any journey of forgiveness is growth and renewed hope. Again, the hope is not necessarily hope to keep living in a marriage where your spouse is continually betraying or abusing you; the hope is an expectation that God is allowing you to forgive so you can anticipate what action He is calling you to in the marriage. Your forgiveness is also a way to free your spouse from your expectation. They must deal with God on the pain they have caused you and if their heart is repentant before God then change should follow.

Conditions of the Heart for Forgiveness

Let's take a look at the conditions of our heart that are necessary for forgiveness.

1. It must come from the heart with compassion

2. It should not measure the size of the debt or limit the action of forgiveness

3. It will involve an action of some kind

This is demonstrated very clearly in the Gospel of Matthew 18. A certain king was owed a very large debt by one of his servants. When his servant appeared before him, he begged for mercy knowing that he could not possibly pay back his debt. The king forgave the debt and erased it completely. The servant then went out and demanded a much lesser amount from one of his debtors and in fact threw that debtor in prison in order to collect his measly debt. When the king heard this, it frustrated him. He called the servant back and said *"You wicked servant! I forgave you all that debt because you begged me, should you not also have had compassion on your fellow servant, just as I had pity on you?" Matthew 18:32b–33* NKJV

Many principles are demonstrated in this parable but the three foundational aspects necessary for true forgiveness are obvious. The king knew he was owed a very large debt, he chose the **condition of his heart** as one of softness and compassion toward the servant. He **didn't consider** how large the debt was but listened to the servant tell of his inability to pay it back. Lastly he **chose an action** of cancelling the entire debt. So we have here an example of true forgiveness. The debt was erased but because the servant who was forgiven did not really understand the forgiveness that was granted him, he was not able to impart forgiveness to his debtor. Again the emphasis is on the heart of those imparting forgiveness. That is what God is concerned about. The person who receives the forgiveness has the choice to make as well but God will deal with them. So Jesus is telling us that forgiveness is not an option, it is an imperative. This parable ends with Jesus telling us that *"So my heavenly Father also will do to you if each of you from his heart does not forgive his brother his trespasses." Matthews18: 35* NKJV

We must understand that forgiveness is directly tied to two things 1.) Our prayers being answered, and 2.) Our acceptance and understanding of Christ's forgiveness. These two factors alone should motivate us to forgive a spouse who hurt us. In this forgiving we must also ask God to show us what action we need to take. If we reflect again on the parable in Matthew 18 the king first chose to take an action of entirely erasing the debt– clean slate– all of it gone. After he granted forgiveness he had an opportunity to observe the reaction of the servant to his forgiveness. He then decided that he would no longer forgive the entire debt, but instead would request full payment.

We might view these actions as contradictory but since we know that the forgiveness was genuine and compassionate with no expectations, the response after the king found out about the servant's hardness of heart was not taking back the forgiveness. He was simply acknowledging the servant's actions and responses and making an informed decision about how to proceed in the relationship. If we have imparted forgiveness to a spouse for a major infraction, and it is from our heart freely given, then we have the freedom to pursue the God led action that will best communicate our forgiveness. If the debtor has a hard heart and cannot really accept that forgiveness and change their behavior, we can be rest assured that God will lead us in the next course of action. This king was able to see the heart of the servant– his entitlement and pride– from how he responded to forgiveness. Because of that he felt freedom to have a different action, different boundary and different expectation of the servant. This is also

> *God allows us to make the hard choice to forgive; He deals with the heart of the person we are forgiving*

a freeing concept about forgiveness, we are only responsible for choosing the action we will follow to forgive–take the spouse back, go to treatment with them, release our bitterness, or so on. We do not assume responsibility for the spouse's reaction to our forgiveness. God allows us to make the hard choice to forgive; He deals with the heart of the person we are forgiving. He does not expect us to forgive with an expectation of how the spouse will change.

That is why forgiveness is really a condition of our heart fully committed to Jesus Christ because it is not possible without His love. We are told in John 15: 9–10 *"As the Father loved me, I also have loved you; abide in My love. If you keep my commandments you will abide in My love, just as I have kept my Father's commandments and abide in His love."* NKJV

This passage clearly tells us that abiding in Christ is done by obeying His commandments. Jesus tells us later in verse 12–13 what His commandment is, *"that you love one another as I Have loved you, greater love has no one than this, than to lay down one's life for his friends."* Forgiveness is laying down our life– it is a sacrifice and it hurts a lot. This is why we must look to our own relationship with Christ first, not what our spouse did to us. Without understanding His love, and abiding or living in fellowship with Him, we will not be able to impart forgiveness to a spouse, the expectation of what they should give us in return will just be too much to bear.

Forgiveness Can Lead to Reconciliation

God will lead us in the path of forgiveness if we allow those three conditions to be present in our heart. The ultimate outcome of true forgiveness working in the hearts of both the giver and the receiver is reconciliation. God gave us the ministry of reconciliation which is essentially us being brought into harmony with God through Christ Jesus. (See passages in Romans 5:6–11, II Corinthians 5:18–19, and Ephesians 2:16) We also have this ministry to impart to those in our life. If we are reconciled to Christ and our spouse is reconciled to Christ then it begs to reason that we can walk in a place of oneness with our spouse in Christ. Reconciliation has been defined in many ways "Bringing others into harmony with God" (AMPLIFIED BIBLE), and "reuniting, bringing together, settling, resolving, mending, understanding, peace, agreement, and harmonizing" (New Oxford American Dictionary). There is hope in forgiveness because when both partners graciously walk in forgiveness they can be in harmony, not perfect, but both committed to a life of forgiveness and hope. Either way, forgiveness is a door to a closer walk with God individually and can be a door to a reunited relationship with your spouse. The reward is inestimable.

How Did We Walk it Out?

Some of the practical ways that Kevin and I walk out forgiveness include sharing our hurts and asking for prayer from each other for painful memories even when we would rather shut down. We also continue to speak the truth to ourselves about our commitment to one another rather than ruminating about how we hurt each other. We pray for one another, especially in areas that we struggle. If Kevin is struggling with being rageful, and this is a reminder for me of the past when I felt scared and on eggshells, I can reach out and ask if I can pray for him. Showing grace to him will help shake me out of my self–pity and into an action that will promote forgiveness. When we were first reconciling and choosing to remarry, we understood that there would be multiple occasions of forgiving and putting out of mind the hurt we had inflicted on one another. When I would shut down and want to be quiet, Kevin could be plagued with fear that I would shut him out and he could never meet my needs, or he could choose to say those words opposite of what he wanted like, "Chris, I want to be a Godly husband to you, but it is hard to know if you are angry at me or not when you shut down." By his choice to speak the truth in love to me, he was choosing a path of forgiveness. Sometimes I would respond with kindness and sometimes I would shut down and not care. The bottom line is that one of us had to make a move towards speaking forgiveness and reaffirming our reconciliation. In doing this the end result was one of us was motivated by hope that we could get through this and we could be restored to one another. When the hand of forgiveness was extended I had an opportunity to respond, just like the servant in Matthew, I could graciously accept the forgiveness, or I could feel entitled to what I was owed.

The Small Things Matter

There are countless ways that we hurt one another in a marriage. Some are the obvious hope busters, some are the passive, inadvertent acts of forgetfulness that compound. These could include:

- We are harsh and don't apologize

- We forget a special occasion

- We don't take the time for our spouse that they need

- We don't help out with the kids the way we could

- We don't notice the little things our spouse does

- We don't touch enough

- We put off the sexual advance of our spouse over and over

- We get busy

- We get selfish

- We get distracted with our own troubles and grief

- We don't respect

- We shut down

- We spend too much money

- We don't treasure one another

- We don't help out in the kitchen

- We grow to expect things like oil changes, dinner, homework, making appointments, lawn care, cleaning the house etc.. are all done by our spouse without a thank you

This is not an exhaustive list but it is a representation of how the little losses, along with the hope busters we identified in chapter two, can foster unforgiveness if not recognized, talked about, and changed. It is important

154

that we are able to see areas that we have hurt our spouse, big and small, so that we may seek forgiveness and change.

None of us is immune to the power of unforgiveness in our marriage, but the good news is that none of is exempt from the goodness of God's grace through the gift of forgiveness to one another. Let's forgive and continue to fuel hope.

Taking it Home

1. What do you think forgiveness really means? Are you a forgiving person or do you hold onto things? Do you have expectations when you forgive? What would some of them be?

2. Do you consider your spouse to be a forgiving person? What would help you realize their forgiveness towards you in a more real way?

3. Are there things you can name that you may be holding back forgiveness from your spouse? What are they?

4. Name some of the smaller things you may not be forgiving your spouse for? Write out your list and then write out how you can talk to your spouse about this in letter or person.

5. Is there something you believe your spouse may be holding against you or not forgiving you for? (Big or small) What is it and what will you do to move towards forgiveness with your spouse?

6. Are there choices, habits, or actions that you have not forgiven yourself for? What are they? Do you need to confess these to someone and seek healing? If so what will you do?

HOPE CHALLENGE

Take the time to write out a forgiveness prayer stating all the hurts and wounds you feel your spouse has done to you. Pray this prayer everyday releasing and forgiving your spouse. If you can pray it together with your spouse that would be ideal but if not then pray it as your own prayer of confession and release.

Example: Father, You know I have been holding unforgiveness towards my spouse for _____. I don't know how to get over it but I want You to hear my prayer and I want to release my spouse from my anger and pain with no more expectations so that You will deal with their heart the way You see fit. Help me identify the attitudes I may have toward my spouse, help me stop doing the behaviors that are hurtful to my spouse. It is by Your grace and forgiveness that I am able to do all things according to your will. I want to be free from unforgiveness and so today I choose to be free from this in Jesus name.

157

Chapter 7 – How Prayer Impacts Your Hope Level

"Pray without ceasing." 1 Thessalonians 5:17 NIV

This chapter is very important in understanding the great power of prayer between a husband and wife. It is also a topic that some people may feel very uncomfortable about, especially if they are not accustomed to praying out loud or in front of people. Our hope is that you will find this chapter relevant to the health of your marriage no matter where you fall in your belief about prayer.

The Hebrew word "yachal" is used for the word hope in Psalms 33:22 *"Let thy mercy, O Lord, be upon us, according as we hope in thee."* KJV

A few of the other words to express hope in this verse are trust, tarry, wait, and be patient. These words are very descriptive when we think about praying and they illuminate how prayer includes waiting on the Lord. David is stating that our hope, or trust level, is directly correlated to God pouring HIS mercy on us. We would go further to say that as we more and more seek God in prayer, we will see an increase in our hope level. I'm sure that David's hope increased as he felt and observed God's mercy in his life. We have this same promise that as we hope in God through prayer and waiting on Him, we can expect His mercy to be poured out in our lives. The hardest part about this idea is that we tend to withdraw from prayer or communication with God as our hope decreases. We see less evidence of God working in our lives

> *We must seek God, humble ourselves, and have a conversation with Him*

with mercy when we feel less hopeful. This is why Kevin and I believe that even in the midst of hell breaking loose and chaos reigning in your home, we must pray. We must seek God, hu4mble ourselves, and have a conversation with Him. We must remind ourselves that our hope is in Him, tell Him that we expect Him to pour out His mercy upon us as we wait and hope in Him. That mercy often times doesn't come in the form we expect. Often the trial is not removed but rather we are given the patience and endurance to walk through the trial. That is the power of expectancy in prayer.

Pray Together

Chris and I see so many couples that don't actively pray together, and most of them say that they were never taught by a parent or mentor to do this, or that they never saw their parents pray together. Children see our example. They learn by watching what we do, more than by listening to what we say. My parents prayed every day before my dad went to work and I know that because of their example, that it really impacted me to understand the power of prayer.

Unfortunately, in our first marriage prayer was used sparingly, and especially if we were in trouble, it was not a definitive part of our experience together as a couple. When we headed towards divorce, prayer was no longer a viable part of our daily life together. We were fighting all the time and spent more time trying to change one another than surrendering our problems to God. I'm not suggesting that our divorce was only because we did not pray together, but our breakdown in the marriage was related to me not fulfilling the role of the spiritual leader, and that includes praying together. I know that if we would have made prayer a priority in the first years of our marriage, things would have been different, and we may have never gotten divorced. Why? Because as we turned our hearts towards God filling us instead of us figuring it all out, we would have been humbled and more willing to seek God instead of our solution to the problem. We may have even been more open to seeking help, spending money on investing in counseling for our marriage, and more realistic about waiting on the Lord instead of trying to get out of our miserable situation.

Faith and Hope Are Intertwined

The power of prayer is spoken of so many times in the Bible. It is the cornerstone of our entire Christian walk. If you think about it, as we are praying and building our faith, we are also building our hope level. Hebrews 11:1 tells us *"To have faith is to be sure of the things we hope for, to be certain of the things we cannot see."* GNB

Faith and hope are intrinsically intertwined. Faith is built from hope and hoping for things is the same as having faith. So again we see that there is an active expectation of something to happen as we hope. This is clear evidence that we are not hoping in vain, or having empty hope for something. We are putting our faith to work as we hope for what God has in store for our marriage.

Answers Are Not Always in Our Time

Take some time to read Daniel 10. This is such a powerful example of the power of our prayers. Understand that Daniel was praying and fasting for 21 days before Gabriel came in the vision. Gabriel made it clear that Daniel's prayers were heard the moment he uttered them. The angel also clarified that it was Daniel's willingness to be humble, in order to

When Chris and I pray together, we are uniting as a couple, in a bond that the enemy cannot break

gain understanding, which caused his prayer to be answered. The angel is speaking of the state of Daniel's heart. He was coming to the Lord in humility, desiring understanding from the Lord. Obviously he prayed with hope and expectancy that he would gain understanding. Imagine how Daniel felt that moment when the angel appeared because of his prayers. The text says that he was overwhelmed to the point of fainting. I can imagine that his hope level increased dramatically when Gabriel appeared and told him that his prayers were heard right away! As we are praying, we need to remember the example of Daniel and understand that God above does hear our pleas. We don't have to understand His timing or how He answers the prayer, we just have to know that He knows, and that is good enough.

In marriage, we know that it is important that our hope level is high, so that we can see the bigger picture at hand. When Chris and I pray together, (and we don't always do it when we are blissful, we do it when we are angry at each other too) we are uniting as a couple, in a bond that the enemy cannot break.

> Matthew 18:20 For where two or three are gathered together in my name, there am I in the midst of

This is a promise couples! Jesus is telling us in the verse above that if we as a couple come together and pray in Jesus' name, that He will come and be in the midst of us. This needs to be so foundational to your marriage. Unfortunately, this is not something that is taught in every pre–marriage class out there, and it should be.

Prayer in the marriage IS ESSENTIAL to the success of healthy Christian marriage, and it is key in building your hope level so that you can see through the trials you will face together. Chris and I have been through some trials throughout our combined18 years of marriage, and I can tell you that the years where we prayed together, were years with more hope and expectancy of God's goodness despite our failings.

Sometimes You Will Have to Make the First Move

Jesus continued to pray even when the disciples fell asleep in the garden. You will probably encounter this in your marriage sometime, and so it is necessary to be prepared to step up and persevere. There have been many times in our marriage where Chris or I have just been stubborn and the other one has had to step up and pray alone for the other no matter how frustrating it can be. One of us has to make the first move and pray or initiate prayer. The key is not getting proud that you are making the first move, and in fact it is a time that you can humbly thank the Lord for working through you in your spouse's life.

> *We are called to sacrifice for our spouse throughout the marriage, giving of ourselves the way Christ did for the church*

We are called to sacrifice for our spouse throughout the marriage, giving of ourselves the way Christ did for the church. It takes hope just to be able to do this, but sacrificing also builds hope as you reflect on how Christ sacrificed for us and how He forgave us at the cross. You can be excited that you are becoming more like Him in your actions. Not so you can be boastful or proud, but so that you can be motivated by your spiritual growth and humbled by God's work in your life, despite your own shortcomings.

You may feel alone in these times, so it is also very important to pray with others that you trust. Praying with a friend during those times of desperation or pain in your marriage will strengthen and empower you to stay strong and receive direction from God about your marriage and your individual responsibility in it. Be sure that your prayer partner is a person who lives by the power of prayer in their own life as well. Being alone and isolating yourself from others during difficult times will draw you away from God's presence and His influence in your life. It is, unfortunately, our first response when we are in pain.

We are Mighty in Prayer

> *James 5:16Confessyour faults one to another, and pray one for another, that ye may be healed. The effectual fervent prayer of a righteous man*

James uses the words "effectual fervent". Energeō is the Greek word used here which means; to *be active, efficient:* do, (be) effectual (fervent), be mighty in, shew forth self, work (effectually in) (Strong's Exhaustive Concordance). I like "be mighty in" because to me it gives a definition of what we can look like in prayer. If God is saying "be mighty in", He is saying that we have authority in Christ when we are praying in HIS name. He uses the word availeth; Ischuō (the Greek word used) means to *have* (or *exercise*) *force* (literally or figuratively): be able, avail, can do, could, be good, might, prevail, be of strength (Strong's Exhaustive Concordance).

So I read it like this: "the *MIGHTY* (an authority based) prayer of a righteous man *WILL FORCE* much." Prayer makes things happen in the spiritual realm.

It is awesome to study the scripture and really ponder what the deep meaning of the word is. It is actually really inspiring and motivating when you see the great depth of the Hebrew and Greek language, and learn how the words are used in the scripture you are studying. Don't be passive and let the enemy tell you prayer is not something you have

> *This is a spiritual inheritance that you are leaving the generations to come*

to do. It bolsters your faith, unites you with your enemies (sometimes that feels like your spouse), and it calls forth legions of heavenly forces to bring help your way. The help may be patience when you need it, a change in attitude, a different circumstance, or maybe just peace in the situation. It doesn't matter what the answer is, just know that God will provide it.

Use Prayer All the Time

Remember how much power your prayer has when you come together as a couple in Jesus' name. HE urges us to use prayer in every situation; there is no time when prayer is not needed in marriage, and it is an asset for your kids (if you have any). When your kids, and anyone else for that matter, see you praying together, they learn by your witness, and then the fruit of that prayer, whether it is answered in a visible form, or if it is answered just by the building of your faith, will shine the light of Jesus to them. This is a spiritual inheritance that you are leaving the generations to come! Let's face it, we need a spiritual inheritance. Our kids need to have the advantage of parents that pray for them and they need to flow in the power of prayer themselves. Chris and I have been so blessed to have children that totally understand why we pray. They are never afraid to ask us to stand with them in prayer or to pray for us.

Don't Hinder Your Prayers

1Peter 3:7 "Ye husbands, in like manner, dwell with your wives according to knowledge, giving honor unto the woman, as unto the weaker vessel, as being also joint–heirs of the grace of life; to the end that your prayers be not hindered." ASV

Here we see that the author is calling us to dwell with our wife in a way that is honorable, to keep in mind that they are not built like us men, and they have qualities that we don't. Then he goes on to say that if we live this way, that our prayers will not be hindered. He is setting up the idea that our treatment of our wives is directly connected to our prayers being heard. Our hearts must always be in a place of humility before the Lord. We must be asking God to hear our prayers of course, but more importantly we must be asking Him to help us treat our wives in a God honoring way. The principle here is critical– our prayer requests and our prayer answers are directly correlated to our honor level in our marriage. Ouch! This is a strong warning and a clear one as well. If I can't even treat my wife the way Christ treats me, how can I expect my prayers to be heard above?

Knowledge Opens the Door to Prayer

Further, we are told to dwell with our wives according to knowledge. Other words for knowledge are familiarity, awareness, understanding, wisdom and skill. These words imply that if you don't know what you need to honor your wife, you need to obtain the skills and understanding to do so. Clearly for some of us that means getting help, counseling, treatment, or support. If we are seeking to have our prayers answered, the imperative in the passage in 1 Peter 3 is to obtain knowledge about our wife, to truly strive to know her, and in doing this you will give her honor. This is indicative that prayer is a process that requires us to give something up, which is not easy for most of us. The thing that we are asked to give up, as husbands, is selfishness. So we must make it our aim to use skill and wisdom to lovingly honor our wives. Most of us approach prayer with an expectation of the outcome. Prayer is the ultimate act of trust and surrender. We are stepping out in obedience, doing what we have been commanded to do, checking our hearts and actions along the way, and then we are falling back into that unknown place of trusting God's sovereignty.

We must grasp the significance of prayer as a tool of our obedience to Christ, and then we must mightily pray expecting to see the results that God has promised us.

Taking it Home

1. What is your comfort level with prayer? Praying with your spouse? Praying during your personal time? What does prayer actually mean to you?

2. Is prayer a part of your relationship with your spouse? Is it something that needs to change in your marriage? In what way does it need to change?

3. Is there a time in your life that you can reflect on where the power of prayer was evident? What was that time and what impact did prayer have on you or your situation?

4. What can you do this week to bring prayer to a new level in your marriage? (be specific, i.e. praying each morning together before work, asking your spouse for their prayer needs.)

HOPE CHALLENGE

This week we want you to think about the power that prayer has to bring hope into your marriage. Be honest with God and let Him know what you need. If you are running on low hope, pray for His strength and wisdom to see the hope in your marriage. Keep in mind that HE is your source of hope, not your spouse, and what they do or how they live does not have to affect your hope level this week, because you are getting it filled by Christ. Decide how you will use prayer in your personal walk and with your spouse in a different way and do it.

Chapter 8 – Leaving a Legacy of Hope for Your Children

*"Praise the LORD! Happy is the person who honors the LORD, who takes pleasure in obeying his commands. The good man's **children** will be powerful in the land; his **descendants** will be blessed. His **family** will be wealthy and rich, and **he** will be prosperous forever." Psalms 112:1 GNB*

Legacy is an important thing to consider. The verses above are a great example of leaving a legacy, especially for your children. If you have the power of hope alive in your life, and in your marriage, then you're giving an irreplaceable gift to your children. What does it mean then to leave a legacy of hope for our children? Is it to leave them a large financial inheritance, a family business to run, vacation properties to hang out at? This may be part of your inheritance but it is not necessarily part of your legacy. Legacy also means heritage, gift, birthright, consequence, and result. I like the word consequence or result. A marriage, where a couple is building upon a foundation of hope, and living out the principles of hope daily will have the consequence, or result, of imparting that same hope to their children. Is this an ironclad promise that our children will not stray, or be unhappy–NO. It is just a way to help us understand that our behaviors today affect our children tomorrow. Our legacy is also a way to affect the consequences of our children's later life experience.

Live by The Word of God

The verse above, Psalms 112:1 tells us "HAPPY" is the person who honors the Lord, who takes pleasure in obeying His commands. This is a very hopeful outcome isn't it? There is a reward for the children and descendants of those that live by the Word of God. Again, there is a corresponding action that we can take that will guarantee that our expectation, or our hope, is met. We can honor the Lord, we can take pleasure in obeying His commands, we can experience a hope–filled life. The verse goes on to tell us more hopeful news; *"The good man's **children** will be **powerful** in the land; his **descendants** will be **blessed**. His **family** will be **wealthy and rich**, and he will be prosperous forever."* GNB

The Greek word for wealth means, to have enough. Isn't that an awesome revelation? Our children can have an expectation or an anticipation of a certain outcome (powerful, blessed, wealthy and rich), based on our choices today to build our lives and our marriages on the hope of Jesus Christ. We are excited to know that our children are being blessed as we grow closer to the Lord.

Choose Life for Your Children

*Deuteronomy 30:19–20 "I call heaven and earth as witnesses today against you, that I have set before you life and death, blessing and cursing: therefore **choose life**, that both you and your descendants may live, that you may love the Lord your God, that you may obey His voice, and that you may cling to Him, for He is your life and the length of your days; and that you may dwell in the land which the Lord swore to your fathers, to Abraham, Isaac, and Jacob to give them." NKJV*

Here, we see a call to choose life for our children (descendants), life and blessing, not death and cursing. When we give into the death of hope in our marriage, we are giving in to a curse in our lives, and ultimately in the lives of our children. Kevin and I had literally lost all hope, there was no expectation, desire, change, or anticipation for anything to be different in our marriage. We were lost and essentially living under a curse. This isn't some super spiritual, how do I figure it out type of curse, this was the "choose life" part of that verse that we failed to do. We did not choose to stop our drinking, our fighting, our stubbornness, our pride and our hurt, we instead chose death; the death of our marriage, the death of our covenant to one another and to God. We were too hopeless with our circumstances to understand that our choices were leaving ripple affects for our son.

Brandon was an amazing little boy, an easy child, and very fun loving. He was also devastated about our split. He had experienced the fights, the yelling, the silence and the space between us for years, but the death blow came when daddy moved out. We chose death and death is what followed in our son's life. He had two homes that he went back and forth between instead of the family home with his cool bedroom. He had to get used to our different lifestyles, relationships, and choices. He had to say goodbye to the feeling of security he had knowing that his parents were together, and trade that in for a life of insecurities, unknowns, and questions about our divorce. We, on the other hand, felt justified in our decision because we were not fighting in front of him. We were finally done trying so hard to please one another and we were able to live for what we wanted. We falsely believed that our choice would bring him a new life since it brought us a new life.

After we decided to reconcile our marriage, Brandon showed me (Chris) some notes he had written during our divorce. They were folded up so tiny hidden away in his room. They said, "God, I wish my parents would get back together," and, "God, why won't my parents stop fighting?" They broke my heart with their rawness and vulnerability. They were the words of a young eight–year old boy trying to understand the death of his parent's marriage. It also reflects his simple, yet profound, understanding of how we had disobeyed God, how we had not chosen life. What a legacy we had left our little boy. We could not stop fighting and chose loss of hope, over true help for ourselves and our marriage.

The Promised Land Requires Action from Us

In the scripture passage in Deuteronomy 30, Moses is laying out a very concise plan for the Israelites to choose life for themselves and their descendants. Not easy but clear. The promised land is an example of the promise of a different life that God has for us, the Israelites are an example to us of a generation of people who had lost hope and faith in God and who wandered aimlessly with no expectation of change. They were living under a curse and therefore were kept in bondage by the Egyptians and by their "slave mentality". When they had the promised land in front of them they still needed instruction on how to pursue it, how to walk in hope. God is telling them here, through Moses, that He keeps his promise to them and their children for an inheritance. He is asking them to do some things though. In verse 20 it states *"that you may love the Lord your God, that you may obey His voice, and that you may cling to Him, for He is your life and the length of your days."* NKJV

So we see three ways that they are asked to serve the Lord:

1.) Love the lord

2.) Obey His Voice

3.) Cling to Him–understand He is your life

Loving Him is taking the time to know His thoughts and His ways. It is being willing to lay down our life for His purposes, to serve Him wherever He may call us. It is seeking Him for the direction our life should go. What Kevin and I failed to do, although we loved God, was ask Him if the divorce was really the best option for our marriage. Obeying God is also taking the time to read His word, seek Him for direction in your life, and conform to His standards of living. For example, since we know "God hates divorce" Malachi 2:16 (NIV) it would have would benefited us to do all we should have done, within our power, to obey His commands prior to the final decision to divorce. Our obedience has a direct result on our descendants.

Clinging to God implies that He is our source. We understand our full

> *We are to be an example of hope to our children so that they too may see life abundantly for generations to come*

dependency on Him. Not because we are incompetent, unintelligent, or incapable but because He is sovereign and wise. Our life source is found in Him and our thankfulness should then overflow in our relationship with Him. We should cling to His truth during the trials rather than rely on our version of what is happening. Again these three actions follow the promise for life for us and our descendants. That is why it is imperative that we seek understanding of how His promises, and our acceptance of them by our action, are so closely related.

We are to be an example of hope to our children so that they too may see life abundantly for generations to come. We know that as we seek Christ in our marriage and life, we are building hope for the future that God promises us. In doing this our children will learn how to build the same hope in their own lives.

> Hebrews 6:18b–19So we who have found safety with him are greatly encouraged to hold <u>firmly to the hope</u> placed before us. We have this <u>hope as an anchor for our lives</u>. It is safe and sure, and goes through the curtain of the heavenly temple into the inner sanctuary. ASV

We promised in the verses above that if we are His children (find safety with Him), that we have access to this hope. Our children have the same opportunity that we do for this hope to be placed before them, within their reach! We read though, that we have to <u>hold firmly</u> to the hope in order to keep it. The only way we can hold firmly to this hope is by being in the word and pursuing Jesus and an authentic relationship with Him. But sometimes, during fights, trials and loss in our marriage, holding firmly feels like a desperate act where we are literally hanging on for dear life to hope, but do not fear it is a promise to you. Reach out to others that can help you during those times of sadness and worry. Just because you cannot feel the hope, does not mean that it is not working. Jesus was raised to life and sits at the right hand of the Father making intercession for you. (See Romans 8:34) You have a full time prayer warrior on your side.

We can literally be anchored or fixed in hope because of our relationship with Jesus Christ. When Jesus died the temple curtain was torn in half (See Hebrews 6:19b). You may not realize that this symbolizes that we now have free access to His gift of salvation and to His promises. We have access to enter into the inner sanctuary, which is the closest place to God in the Old Testament. This is a place where we access His promises. We don't have to bring a sacrifice, (good works) we don't have to have it all together. We just have to come with a willingness to obey His voice; His promise is Hope. Jesus fulfilled that hope by dying on the cross and forgiving us of all our sins. He gave us a promise as His children; we too can give our children a promise of hope by leaving an example and a legacy for them to follow.

We Have to Teach Our Children

So how do we teach our children to walk in hope? Being in the Word so that we can understand how to lead by the example of the Bible is number one. The Bible is our guide book and it is loaded with the tools to help us walk a Christ-centered walk. As our children see us practicing what we learn, they will naturally want to follow. It is important to recognize that children do react differently to teaching and correction. If the teaching is more like the law, you may experience rebellion from your kids. The more real you are, letting them see your weaknesses, the easier it is to teach them. Kids need to know that you are imperfect, and that you too experience trials in life, so that they may learn from your mistakes.

This is where you have to choose to be vulnerable about your mistakes and errors as a parent, and seek the forgiveness of your children when you have wronged them.

Different Approaches Elicit Different Responses From our Kids

As parents we usually have different approaches to teaching and correcting our children. Some of us use a more grace, sometimes permissive, based approach; while some are more comfortable using legalism, control, and correction. God calls us to balance in parenting and that is why both parents have a very specific role to fulfill and why we need to honor the role that each of us has. A particular example in our lives happened when Brandon was around 13. He was interested in listening to some secular music bands and I approached it with more of a "do what I say" mentality, and Chris, having a different understanding and more education on child rearing, approached it a little more realistically. She listened to him better, and asked him about his feelings on the matter. She also encouraged him to study out the lyrics and the lifestyles of the bands and see what he came up with. I was very adamant with my position and really stuck to my guns for a while. Often I was dominant and somewhat bossy about my position. One day Chris approached me in love, and with respect, and challenged me to put a little slack on my approach to this topic. I listened to her, even though I felt I was right, and I was amazed that as I gave Brandon freedom and responsibility, for his own choices, he made choices that I respected. I stopped putting my hope in him doing what I said and I started putting my hope in Christ and His leading in my life as a father. If I could lead with love and compassion, stating my expectations for Brandon, I could anticipate (hope) and trust that God was working in Brandon's life to help him make the best decisions.

In the end, Brandon ended up having a great passion for Christian music and though he does like some secular bands, I could see that as I allowed him to make choices with his own conviction, he actually grew closer to God. I was always very clear about my own standards, and what we would and would not allow into our house. In doing this, he could see our values and he really did respect where we were coming from. He could also see our foundation of hope. We knew that we could trust in and expect God to do great things in us and in our children, so we didn't have to control the outcome. We could trust God to do the work. This is not easy to do and is impossible if you do not have hope present in your marriage. How can you allow freedom to your children in certain areas if you are still trying to control the outcome or response of your spouse?

> *When we give our kids the opportunity to make good choices for their lives, rather than just dictating what has to happen, they mature and learn what great responsibility comes with making the right choice*

HE Does the Work, You Obey

Again we see that understanding God's grace is the key element in appreciating the power of hope to leave a legacy for your children. He does the work, you take the steps of obedience with a heart of humility. If you are trying to control, or irrationally disciplining your children, they too will lose hope: the results are disastrous. When we give our kids the opportunity to make good choices for their lives, when they are developmentally responsible to understand those choices, rather than just dictating what has to happen; they mature and learn what great responsibility and reward comes with making the right choices. They are then filled with hope that they are capable and responsible individuals. If they make the wrong choices, use it as a teachable moment to help guide them back to truth and hope.

Now, understand that we also need to have boundaries with our kids. Some choices and expectations have to be set by the parents. However, as you give your children more and more responsibility with positive results, this will enable them to trust your direction and

> *As you give your children more and more responsibility, with positive results, this will enable them to trust your direction and your example.*

your example. This also leaves them with the hope that they are capable, smart people with the ability to affect change in their life. If all they experience is parents that just tell them what to do without a chance to screw up at times, there is little room for hope that life is different out in the world. They should be motivated by that same desire we talked about in chapter one– the desire for change. That only comes from needing something to change and being aware of it. Remember if our children experience a sense of hopelessness in their life with us, a sense that they are trapped, controlled and unable to change because of their parent's expectation; they will be unable to anticipate anything other than that in their adult life.

Looking back, we are so proud of the decisions that Brandon has made for his life despite our failures. We also know that if we would have tried to dictate the outcome of his choices, he would have had a more difficult time respecting our example. More importantly, our decision to reconcile and rebuild a marriage that was by all accounts dead, has given him such hope and promise of what God is capable of doing. We can see the legacy of hope that is being left for him and for our girls now. Not because we are perfect, but because we keep believing and hoping that God will change us, help us, and enable us to be all that He has called us to be. We believe now in the inheritance that our children will experience because of our choices, and so we make these choices more carefully and with less selfishness.

Use the *Word* to Give Hope

We see also in the Bible the responsibility we have as parents to teach our children by the Word, so that they will reap the benefits of the promises that God made to them as His children.

"But his delight is in the law of Jehovah; And on his law doth he meditate day and night. And he shall be like a tree planted by the streams of water, That bringeth forth its fruit in its season, Whose leaf also doth not wither; And whatsoever he doeth shall prosper." Psalms 1:2–3 ASV

Do not get discouraged in your parenting role. It can be tiring and sometimes without immediate rewards. Like a tree, however, it will bring forth fruit in the right season. As parents we naturally want to see everything go well with our kids, hoping that they don't have to go through the same struggles that we endured. This is understandable, but not realistic. Many of us, including myself had parents that left a legacy, and I still had to go through certain trials and even make some very bad mistakes in life before I understood my responsibility to build upon that legacy of hope. The key phrase here is, "that bringeth forth its fruit in its season." As we put our kids in God's hands, from the day they are born, we are allowing that season to be in His timing! This is so important to understand friends, because so many times it is easy to try to take the reins back from God, and this does not work. We are called to be the example for our children, in our walk with Christ, in our marriage, and in our pursuit of hope in all we do. Let your legacy to your children be one of hopefulness.

Taking it Home

1. In what way have you left a legacy of hope for your children? What behaviors, routines, or habits do you practice as an individual, and in your marriage, that are instilling hope in them?

2. Are there situations with your kids that feel hopeless to resolve? What are they? What behaviors or choices are you doing that may contribute to the hopelessness of the situation? What are some possible strategies that you could try that may help?

3. Do you think your kids are hopeful? What would it look like to have a hopeful child? What would they act like in their teenage years? As an adult?

4. What would a balanced approach to discipline look like to you? An approach that would impart

hope to your child but would still have boundaries and expectations? In what ways do you and your spouse balance one another in parenting? In what ways do you want to balance one another better?

HOPE CHALLENGE

Sit down with your spouse this week and write out what you want to see changed in your parenting style. Make a goal to tackle one of those items at a time. While you are at it, approach your child (ren) this week in a totally different manner than you normally would and tell them what you admire and love about them (take them out to breakfast, write a letter, sit down with them, or draw a picture). Try to write out specific traits or personality qualities that you love.

Chapter 9 – Hope Leads To Change

"Then Jesus spoke to them again, saying, I am the light of the world. He who follows Me shall not walk in darkness, but have the light of life." John 8:12 NKJV

*"Fear not for I am with you; Be not dismayed, for I am your God. I will strengthen you, Yes I will **help** you, I will uphold you with my righteous right hand. "Isaiah 41:10 NKJV*

"In the day when I cried out, you answered me, and made me bold with strength in my soul." Psalms138:3 NKJV

*"Our soul waits for the Lord; He is our **help** and our shield." Psalm 33:20 NKJV*

Hope has the power to bring healing and change into any marriage, but how does it do that? Just because we understand that hope is related to spiritual leadership, forgiveness, and prayer doesn't necessarily mean that we will know what to do with that information. Ultimately, it all comes back to a foundational understanding of our own personal relationship with Christ. Jesus gave us the ultimate hope, the hope of eternal life in Him. Let's face it, the entire Christian existence is based on faith; faith that the work done at the cross, and fulfilled through the resurrection, is the only way to heaven. We believe that Satan was defeated through the death and resurrection of Jesus and that he is forever under the feet of Jesus. So from the day we asked Him into our hearts to be our Savior, we made a conscious choice to hope in Him for our life and our salvation. This is, in essence, the simplicity of our hope as individual followers of Christ.

So what we must learn to do is live in such a way that our hope in Christ spills over into every area of our life, and most especially in our marriage. If we allow that hope to influence this sphere of our life, we will know when change, or even help, is needed in our marriage. We will not be bound by our stubbornness, pride, and self-sufficiency to make our marriage work. We will aim to bring the light of God's hope, truth, and freedom into the darkest most wounded part of our marriage, as well as use the tool of hope to bring laughter, joy, and peace into our marriage.

> *From the day we asked Him into our hearts to be our Savior, we made a conscious choice to hope in Him for our life and our salvation*

Let's examine Romans 2:4–8

"Or do you despise the riches of His goodness, forbearance and longsuffering, not knowing that the goodness of God <u>leads</u> you to repentance? But in accordance with your hardness and your

*impenitent heart you are treasuring up for yourself wrath in
the day of wrath and revelation of the righteous judgment of
God, who will render to each one according to his deeds: eternal
life to those who by patient continuance in doing good seek for
glory, honor and immortality, but to those who are self seeking
and do not obey the truth but obey unrighteousness–
indignation and wrath."* NKJV

This is a complex scripture in many ways but it gives
us the foundation for salvation– our great hope and it
further explains that when we reject hope, our actions
end up reflecting that. However, when we embrace that
hope, we seek change. So we will use this foundational
scripture to examine four points. If these points are
properly understood they may open your eyes to the
changes you and your spouse need to make in your
marriage.

1. Understand God's nature

2. Understand your sinful nature

3. Understand how His nature can motivate you
   to seek change

4. Understand how your sinful nature may
   prevent you from pursuing change

Understand God's Nature

God's nature, according to the text in Romans, is one
of goodness, forbearance, and longsuffering. The word
goodness in this text is talking about God's kindness and
integrity when dealing with us as humans. He is good to

us by giving us nature, food, provision, and a world to enjoy. He is good to us because He gives us His grace. Most of us just take those things for granted. We have learned to expect that the goodness of God is a given and we are hard pressed to thank Him for the simple things in life.

The word forbearance means to hold back or exercise restraint. What is God holding back? His judgment for our hardness of hearts and our sinful nature. God could impute justice against us with a flash and yet because of His forbearance, He is restraining Himself from judgment so that we as sinners may have time to come to Him. Again, we often take this aspect of God's nature for granted. We keep saying grace, grace, grace and yet sometimes we are continuing in sin; knowing it is wrong but still taking advantage of God's forbearance.

To be long suffering is to have the ability to suffer for a long period of time. The suffering is not an actual physical suffering but more of a waiting for a long time while watching a lot of painful events occur around you. God's long suffering has been well documented in the Bible. He suffered long while He called the Israelites out of Egypt. He watched them wander, complain and miss the promised land for years (Exodus). He suffered long in the days of Noah when he finally decided to save only Noah and his family and wipe out the rest of the world with a flood (Genesis), and he suffered long with the people of Nineveh while he waited for Jonah to get over his fear and go and tell the people the good news (Jonah). God has the ability to wait a lot longer than we do. He suffers long while waiting for humanity to repent from their sinful ways.

Although this is not an exhaustive list of God's character, we must understand who HE is. Why? Because it is His kindness that leads us to repentance. So understanding the nature of God is your first step towards change. For without comprehending the magnanimous nature of God we can never be truly repentant or be sorry for our own sins. And without being truly sorry for our own sins, and in a place of humility, we will experience difficulty being gracious towards what we perceive as an "unworthy" spouse. Then we will not be able to change our reactions and attitudes towards them because we will be too focused on their wrongdoings.

Understand Your Sinful Nature

It is within our sinful nature to have a hard and impenitent (refusal to repent) heart. We are all sinners saved by grace (See Romans 3:23–24). Some of us may think that we are good people and that we do good things, but the harsh reality is that none of us can boast in our own greatness. No amount of works will get us to heaven. Most of us are self–seeking and living for our own good. By doing this, we are storing up for ourselves wrath–or judgment– that is until Jesus Christ took our place and our punishment. Now we have been made new.

2 Corinthians 5:17 "Therefore if any man is in Christ, he is a new creation, old things have passed away, behold all things have become new." NKJV

If we claim to walk with Christ and to be His follower then our old nature is passed or gone, we are able to take on the qualities of God through His power. Why then in marriages do we see so much hardness of heart, stubbornness, and lack of humility? Because we are in a battle with our old nature. Understand my friend, that your nature (personality), your skills, and your tactics may not bring the result you want in your marriage; especially if you are stubbornly trying to change your spouse out of your own might. The changes we need in our spouse come through the work of Jesus Christ and the conviction of the Holy Spirit.

So stop and ask yourself, "Am I walking in love toward my spouse, not in my old nature?" Are you still relating to your spouse the way you always have? This whole business about old things being passed away is talking about the very essence of who we are. We are not

> *Are you still relating to your spouse the way you always have?*

robots, but we should be mindful that our sin nature always wants to be out on top and ruling in our marriage. We will always want to impose our views, opinions, or rights on our spouse because we are of a fallen nature. The key for us is to be sure that we are assuming the character and attributes of God when we interact with our spouse. Understanding who we are, and where we have come from is another key to accessing hope. Why? Once we understand our need for God because of our fallen nature, we will seek Him for everything and humbly ask Him to change us. The understanding of our sinful nature allows us to seek change and help within ourselves first, rather then putting the blame or responsibility on our spouse. Someone has to make the first move– why not let it be you? Put the old nature to death and try something God wants you to do.

Understand How His Nature Can Motivate YOU to Seek Change

Let's look closely at our text in Romans 2:6b–7 *"Who will render to each one according to his deeds: eternal life to those who by patient continuance in doing good seek for glory, honor, and immortality."* NKJV

This sounds pretty complicated but not if we break it down. What Paul, the author, is basically telling us is that God has a reward for our good deeds. Don't read this wrong and think you must do good deeds to get to heaven, that is not what is being said. The Word is saying that our final judgment as believers will be a judgment based on our deeds done on this earth while in Christ. The understanding here is that we are motivated to do good works because of God's goodness towards us, we are not motivated out of a false sense of our unworthiness and our need to earn God's love. God is promising us that eternal life is ours if we <u>continue </u>(live) in patience and in doing good for His honor.

No other place is this needed more than in our marriage. How many of you try so hard to make an impression at work? At church? Among your friends? Then we come home and we let it all hang out. We don't exercise patience or goodness. We are not living Christ like lives in our homes. We excuse our behavior by saying that we are tired, we can't trust our spouse, there is too much hurt between us, they don't respect us, and the list goes on. If we have the nature, and the hope of Christ, then every one of these obstacles can be changed. No, we did not say that your spouse will change, we said these obstacles can be changed. Remember we are talking about how His nature can motivate YOU to seek change.

Look again at the text. We are rewarded for our righteous deeds–are we righteous in our marriages or do we write our spouse off? Do we stop trying because we believe they will never change? Do we treat them harshly and unfairly? Do we judge them if they don't live up to our standard of what a spouse should look like? Do we harbor unforgiveness? If so, we are not continuing in patience, or seeking God's good and glory. This is not an old–fashioned guilt trip meant to motivate you to change your ways, this is God's wake up call to get us motivated to do His will. This is also not an excuse for your spouse's blatantly wrong sins or actions towards you. If you have read the entire book you realize that the message of hope is meant to start with one. The ultimate goal is that it is lived out by two. We must look to ourselves first and ask God what changes we can make, especially if our spouse is unwilling or unrepentant. The case with Kevin and I was that we were both motivated for change. We made a plan together and we committed to it. We both were striving to live our lives by walking out our faith and hope towards one another. Don't give up hope that you will not share the vision with your spouse, just do your part and trust God to do His.

So the message is clear, don't just say you believe in the hope of Jesus in your marriage, without showing your hope through action.

James 1:22 tells us *"But be doers of the word and not hearers only deceiving yourselves" NKJV*, and James 2:14,*"What does it profit my brethren if someone says he has faith but does not have works? Can faith save him? If a brother or sister is naked and destitute of daily food and one of you says to them depart in peace, be warmed and filled, but you do not give them the things which are needed for the body, what does it profit? This also faith by itself, if it does not have works, is dead."* NKJV

Know God and let your relationship with Him change and motivate you in your marriage. Don't just believe and hope for change; follow it up with the works. If you have lost your faith and your hope for change, you must start to anticipate, desire, or expect something different. There are times in our marriage where one of us has to step out first and choose a reaction or behavior that is uncomfortable for us in order to build our hope. Do the things you know you must do to start effecting change. Don't stand still, start somewhere. Here are a few ideas that have helped other couples. Only you and your spouse can identify what changes need to happen for you.

- Seek counseling
- Attend church
- Go to treatment
- Stop using silent treatment
- Start the journey of forgiveness
- Start exercising
- Stop drinking
- Stop yelling at the kids
- Start making love to your spouse more
- Talk more
- Yell less
- End that relationship with that "friend" of the opposite sex at work or online
- Stop spending money
- Get out of that adulterous relationship and tell your spouse
- Confront issues
- Start helping around the house
- Work less
- Budget better
- Shop less
- Stop being harsh
- Touch more
- Laugh more
- Take care of yourself
- Eat better
- Stop controlling
- Stop nagging

- Stop being hard on the kids
- Pray together
- Pray alone
- Stop looking at pornography
- Stop watching so much TV
- Stop cutting each other down
- Go on a date
- Go to a marriage conference
- Write a love note to your spouse
- Cook dinner
- Do the laundry
- Say thank you
- Plan a vacation
- Stand up for each other with the kids
- Give a back rub
- Buy them a gift
- Go for a walk together
- Stop being self–sufficient–ask for help
- Stand up to the in–laws
- Apologize and ask forgiveness
- Write a poem to your spouse
- Take a class together
- Praise and compliment your spouse
- Read the Bible

- Start a couple's devotional together

- Don't say "I told You so"

- Buy them a card

- Smile more

- Be on time

Don't allow yourself to get exhausted looking at these ideas and don't convince yourself that you have tried everything and that no one understands how difficult your spouse is. The truth is Kevin and I stop and ask ourselves if we have tried all we can in the relationship to bring hope to our spouse, unfortunately the answer is usually a "no". What typically happens with us is one of us is trying pretty hard at communication, listening, and understanding and we get worn out. The lack of reciprocity can tempt us to wonder, what's the point? It is compounded exponentially when you have had to recover from a major hope buster that has left residual affects of strain on your relationship. You then have a choice to slip back into remembering the past and adopting the old ways of thinking and relating.

It is easier to resent a spouse who is changing slowly, or who has the more obvious change to make. The good news is if you are working together on change, but trying to focus on yourself through the process, then there will be forward movement in your relationship. If you are working on your changes with a non–committal spouse there will also be forward movement–it just may look different. Both scenarios are a win–win. We all have to keep fresh ideas on hand, or at least know the ideas, that will lull us out of our frustration and help us regain perspective. Know God and allow His nature and His love for you to fill you with hope, and motivate you towards change.

Understand How Your Sinful Nature May Prevent You From Pursuing Change

Romans 2:8 *"but to those who are self seeking and do not obey the truth but obey unrighteousness—indignation and wrath."*
NKJV

The verse above is describing the person who is allowing their sinful nature to control them. Clearly we see that they are self–seeking, do not obey the truth, and are unrighteous. If you find yourself continually being selfish in your relationship it is time to ask God to fill you with His nature. This self–seeking behavior may not always be as blatant as we suspect. Many of us as Christians have learned to be self–seeking in ways that do not catch attention. We use body language like eye rolls or a huff of the breath, we expect our spouse to remember certain things without us telling them like an anniversary or birthday, we sit quietly hoping our spouse will notice us in our frustration. The list goes on. It is hard not to seek your own needs above the needs of your spouse especially if you are the one who has been hurt. I can't imagine how Jesus felt when He had to carry HIS cross all alone on the dusty road headed towards His death.

Sometimes I feel ashamed at how self–seeking I am. When I reflect on our first marriage I embodied self–seeking in so many ways. I expected Kevin to be able to read my mind half the time. I felt if he really knew me he should be able to sense things. I also felt like if he didn't totally understand my childhood pain that he was a bad husband. He didn't have any idea how to reach out to me, how could he? I just expected that he should be sensitive and want to ask me questions and help me walk through pain. I didn't think about the fact that I needed to let him know where I was at or what I felt. If he didn't hold me when I cried then I perceived him as a horrible husband. There were so many expectations that I had in the marriage. Some may sound normal to you, as you read this, and yet at the core of all of them was my own self–seeking. I just wanted to be happy and I wanted him to make me happy.

Like we stated earlier, happiness can be a natural byproduct of two people pursuing hope and fullness in Jesus Christ, but the measure of true hope is the changes within your own heart and life, not the performance of your spouse to your expectations.

Recognize Your Own Sins

You must be diligent to recognize the works of the flesh in your life. Kevin and I became lazy in our pursuit of God. We let the little things slip in and we were deceived by the desires of this world. We can recognize these changes by taking an honest inventory of our choices. Where we spend our time, our money, our thoughts, and our energy is usually a good indication of how self–seeking we are. Look at *Galatians 5:19–22, "Now the works of the flesh are evident, which are adultery, fornication, uncleanness, lewdness, idolatry, sorcery, hatred, contentions, jealousies, outbursts of wrath, selfish ambitions, dissensions, heresies, envy, murders, drunkenness, revelries, and the like; of which I tell you beforehand, just as I told you in time past, that those who <u>practice</u> such things will not inherit the kingdom of God."* NKJV

Don't panic if you have committed one or many of these sins, the key word in this phrase is "practice." This is a Greek verb, which is describing continual habitual action. If any of these describe your lifestyle choices, take the time to repent and change. Turn away from the action, don't convince yourself that you can compromise secretly because it won't affect your spouse. It is impossible to invest 100% in a marriage when you are distracted with your own selfish pursuits and sins.

So we see how understanding these four factors can release us into a God given hope within our marriage. The road to change is not easy. In fact, it has been one of the most difficult journeys we have embarked on. Sometimes you may question how you will know if you are walking a path of change and living in hope. Galatians 5:22–25 will always inspire you to measure yourself against the standard Christ has for us, *"But the fruit of the Spirit is love, joy, peace, longsuffering, kindness, goodness, faithfulness, gentleness, self–control. Against such there is no law. And those who are Christ's have crucified the flesh with it's passions and desires. If we live in the Spirit, let us also walk in the Spirit."* NKJV

Sometimes our tendency is to read that and see the words; crucify, flesh, passions, and desires, and get overwhelmed with how much we have to give up.

Obedience is Better Than Sacrifice

I've started to look at this differently. I take each of these fruits and I see myself being in relationship with Kevin and my kids using these fruits. Then I ask myself "What would I look like in conversation with Kevin using self–control instead of losing my temper?" Once I envision the end result, I really like what I see in myself. I see that the fullness Christ intended for me, and for you, can be achieved through obedience. To just stop addictive behavior, halt spending money, or committing adultery out of obligation is a burden. Choices for change made out of obligation will not last. I Samuel 15:22 challenges us *"What is more pleasing to the Lord your burnt offerings and sacrifices or your obedience to His voice? Obedience is far better than sacrifice."* NLT

You may be doing what you think is right in your relationship with your spouse but your approach may be wrong. Just like in the passage of scripture in I Samuel, Saul thought he was doing what was right for the Lord by keeping all the plunder for the Lord. God had told him that he must obey the directions he received through the prophet Samuel, he instead chose a different path. I would encourage you to read this entire passage to understand the power of obedience. The point is you must obey and pursue change in your marriage if you know that it is out of sync with God's intended plan. Suffering through silence, not confronting issues, and running to addiction or adultery are not modes of changing a hopeless marriage. Step out and obey, find the strategy, plan or intervention your marriage needs that will bring hope. Your obedience to pursue change will revolutionize your marriage.

If you are alone; either abandoned, or in a separation, pray for the heart of your spouse. Hardness of heart has destroyed many marriages including ours in the past. Pray Ezekiel 36:26–27 *"I will give you a new heart and put a new spirit within you; I will take the heart of stone out of your flesh. I will put my Spirit within you and cause you to walk in My statutes, and you will keep My judgments and do them."* NKJV

God's promises of hope are for all His children.

Hope leads to change. This statement is your challenge. In your marriage it is time to identify where real change needs to happen. You have a road map. Start with pursuing a full–fledged relationship with Jesus Christ and then identify the specific behavioral, emotional, and spiritual changes you can make. Pray that God will reveal to you the marriage changes that will bring results and stand on the promise of hope found in II Chronicles 7:14 *"If my people who are called by my name will humble themselves and pray and seek my face, and **turn** from their wicked ways, then I will hear from Heaven and forgive their sin and heal their land."* NKJV

Taking it Home

1. Over the last 8 chapters, how have you seen your hope being built? What corresponding changes do you want to make in your marriage, or in yourself, to build upon this foundation?

2. Are there still aspects of your sinful nature that affect your interaction with your spouse? What are they? What could you do differently?

3. How obedient are you to the voice of God in your life and marriage? In what ways do you see yourself as being obedient to Him in serving or ministering to your spouse?

4. Are there long–term changes that need to happen in your marriage to bring more hope? What are they? What is your plan or strategy to bring change to bear in your marriage?

HOPE CHALLENGE

Look at the list on pages 204–207, pick out at least two things you could commit to do with or for your spouse, or for the betterment of your marriage. Commit to making these habits for life. Start today. Expand on the list as you accomplish the goals you set.

Conclusion

Writing this book has been such a blessing for us to do together. We are hopeful that the contents of it will be an asset to all that read it. We pray that you have a life changing encounter with God that will impact you to pursue change in your marriage like never before.

If you are not currently married, we pray you are now armed with the knowledge of what foundation you need to build a marriage upon. If you are fairly content in your marriage we pray this book has motivated you to look deeper below the surface and always build on that foundation of hope. If you are in a marriage that seemed hopeless, we believe that you can take these tools and apply them in your own marriage and rebuild hope. The key is commitment. If you have gone through divorce and need healing in your life, we pray that you have found the tools to begin the healing process and start to build on a new foundation of hope.

Remember that Jesus is the center of our hope and we can always rely on Him to help us build upon it. Our spouse cannot be the source of this hope, but can be impacted greatly as they watch us look to Jesus for our strength and refuge. Remember every marriage starts with a purpose–

define your purpose today. Every marriage is fueled by a vision– what is your vision for your marriage? And every vision is fulfilled through hope. Make an effort today to live in a hope filled marriage.

Appendix

About the Authors

Kevin is an entrepreneur and has owned and operated six different companies. He is a dreamer capable of making his dreams reality, as well as a visionary who has achieved many of his personal and business life goals. He is an avid outdoorsman and elk hunter who raised elk in the past. While he has no formal education in counseling, he does have much experience as a small group leader, Bible study leader, marriage group leader, and conference host and speaker. He desires for men to become in tune with themselves and able to be honorable and respectable, not just in their business lives, but more importantly in their homes as the spiritual leader.

In 1998, he had a miraculous recovery from alcoholism and a selfish lifestyle. He was a broken person who was at the end of his rope and turned to God for his lifeline. Since that time he has battled to put a life of rage, selfishness, and complacency behind him. He fought the battle to win his ex–wife back like a true warrior, but came to a point where he knew that because he had walked out on her he may end up living without her. He persevered with the help of many praying people, and eventually won her over. He has spent the last ten years relentlessly pursuing real life lasting change within himself by dedicating himself to be a protector, a provider, and a defender of his family. He is a work in progress and is dedicated to a lifestyle of honor.

Christine has a Master's degree in social work with an emphasis on family counseling, and has training as mediator, arbitrator, and family group conference leader. She has a variety of work experience including probation officer for domestic abuse and sexual abuse cases. She was also a guardian for neglected and abused children in the system as well as a teacher and presenter for a parents' divorce class. She has conducted multiple parenting assessments and evaluations, developing and recommending parenting plans to the court on behalf of parents. Her work experience is extremely diverse and has exposed her to multiple family issues. She has served alongside Kevin in leading small groups, Bible studies, and hosting conferences. She desires for women to find true security in a relationship with Christ and to realize that their identity does not come from feeling loved or feeling romantic, but from being true to whom God has created them to be.

In 1998, she had to battle with alcohol and depression and it felt like a losing battle. Unlike Kevin, she did not have a miraculous recovery and faced many years of fighting with her thoughts, unhealthy patterns, and expectations and her bent toward intellectualizing and analyzing her life events. She came to a point where she realized that her childhood pain, along with her devastating life choices had caused her to retreat into a shell of a hard, angry, closed person. With lots of unconditional love, support and counseling; she is a person dedicated to maintaining her God given strengths and talents, while being a woman of humility who serves her family in love.

In June 2008, we moved to a 35 acre plot of land north of Canon City, Colorado to build a retreat home dedicated to the ministry of marriage reconciliation. The vision is for Mountain Haven Marriage Ministry and Reconciliation Home to officially open the doors of the ministry home in 2009. Currently we are in the process of getting plans drawn for this retreat home. God is bringing all the details together to make this dream, that we were given over seven years ago, a true reality.

Ideas to Strengthen Your Marriage

1. Attend church regularly

2. Attend Christian or Bible based counseling together or separate

3. Schedule a regular date night where you have fun and don't talk about issues

4. Attend a men's or women's group

5. Attend a small group together

6. Schedule a certain amount of time together face to face to talk as a couple

7. Get away without children–trade babysitting with another couple

8. Write a budget together

9. Have a family game night

10. Pray together daily

11. Evaluate the place alcohol has in your marriage and set standards to live by

12. Write a loving letter or card to your spouse periodically

13. Evaluate the peer relationships you have to make sure that they contribute positively towards your marriage

14. Write out how you will discipline the children so you are both consistent.

15. Get help for yourself if you are wounded or have issues from your past that affect you. Don't wait on your spouse to help you.

16. Attend marriage conferences together or read marriage books together

17. Do a hobby together

Resources to Consider

Torn Asunder: Recovering From Extramarital Affairs by Dave Carder

Love and Respect by Dr. Emerson Eggerichs

Cracking the Communication Code by Dr. Emerson Eggerichs

The Five Love Languages by Gary Chapman

How Can I Forgive You? by Janis Abrams

Love Must Be Tough by Dr. James Dobson

Boundaries in Marriage by Drs. Henry Cloud and John Townsend

Wild at Heart by John Eldredge

Sacred Marriage by Gary Thomas

After the Affair by Janis Abrams

Loving Your Marriage Enough to Protect It by Jerry B. Jenkins

Healing the Hurt in Your Marriage by Dr. Gary and Barbara Rosberg

The Invisible Bond by Barbara Wilson

Marriage on the Rock by Jimmy and Karen Evans

Can My Marriage Be Saved? By Mae and Erika Chambers

Any books by Gary Smalley

Books by Les and Leslie Parrott

References

All Scriptural Quotations were taken from

The Life Recovery Bible– New Living Translation (NLT) Copyright © 1998 by Tyndale house Publishers, Inc., Wheaton, Illinois 60189. Used by Permission. All rights reserved.

The ` MacArthur Study Bible Revised and Updated Edition–New King James Version copyright © 1997 by Word Publishing a division of Thomas Nelson, Inc. Scripture taken from the New King James Version is Copyright © 1979, 1980, 1982 by Thomas Nelson, Inc. Used by permission. All rights Reserved.

The HOLY BIBLE, NEW INTERNATIONAL VERSION ®. Copyright © 1973, 1978, 1984 International Bible Society. Used by permission of Zondervan. All rights reserved.

The Message Bible. Copyright © 1993, 1994, 1995, 1996, 2000, 2001, 2002. Used by permission of NavPress Publishing Group.

Good News Bible in Today's English Version – Second Edition, Copyright © 1992 by American Bible Society. Used by Permission

The King James Version Outside of the United Kingdom, the KJV is in the public domain. Within the United Kingdom, the rights to the KJV are vested in the Crown.

The American Standard Version Thomas Nelson & Sons first published the American Standard Version in 1901. This translation of the Bible is in the public domain.

Other References:

New Oxford American Dictionary Copyright © 2001, 2006, Oxford University Press

The Webster's New College Dictionary Copyright © 2007 by Wiley Publishing, Inc., Cleveland, Ohio

The New Strong's Exhaustive Concordance Copyright © 1995, 1996 by Thomas Nelson Publishers Nashville, TN

15612255R00117

Made in the USA
Lexington, KY
06 June 2012